The Smell of Sin

and the Fresh Air of Grace

DON EVERTS

InterVarsity Press
Downers Grove, Illinois

InterVarsity Press
P.O. Box 1400, Downers Grove, IL 60515-1426
World Wide Web: www.ivpress.com
E-mail: mail@ivpress.com

InterVarsity Press® is the book-publishing division of InterVarsity Christian Fellowship/USA®, a student movement active on campus at hundreds of universities, colleges and schools of nursing in the United States of America, and a member movement of the International Fellowship of Evangelical Students. For information about local and regional activities, write Public Relations Dept., InterVarsity Christian Fellowship/USA, 6400 Schroeder Rd., P.O. Box 7895, Madison, WI 53707-7895, or visit the IVCF website at <www.ivcf.org>.

Unless otherwise noted, Scripture quotations are the author's paraphrase.

Scripture quotations marked NRSV are from the New Revised Standard Version of the Bible, copyright 1989 by the Division of Christian Education of the National Council of the Churches of Christ in the USA. Used by permission. All rights reserved.

Design by Cindy Kiple

Cover images: pollution: Planet Earth/David E. Rowley/Getty Images
             cloud: Akira Kaede/Getty Images

ISBN 0-8308-2389-1
Printed in the United States of America ∞

Library of Congress Cataloging-in-Publication Data
Everts, Don, 1971-
   The smell of sin: and the fresh air of grace / by Don Everts.
     p. cm.
   ISBN 0-8308-2389-1 (pbk.:alk. paper)
   1. Jesus Christ—Teachings. 2. Sin—Biblical teaching. I. Title
BS2417.S52 E94 2003
241'.3—dc21

                                                           2002014456

| **P** | 16 | 15 | 14 | 13 | 12 | 11 | 10 | 9 | 8 | 7 | 6 | 5 | 4 | 3 | 2 | 1 |
| **Y** | 15 | 14 | 13 | 12 | 11 | 10 | 09 | 08 | 07 | 06 | 05 | 04 | 03 | | | |

So let us lay aside

all these sins

which cling so closely.

And let us run with perseverance

the race that is set before us—

ever looking to Jesus,

the pioneer and perfecter of our faith.

Hebrews 12:1-2

Contents

Why You Shouldn't
Read This Book

I have come that you might have life.
JOHN 10:10

This is a book about sin.

I do realize that sin is not our favorite topic these days. It's far from it in fact, and probably for good reasons. For starters, we sin. A lot. Often in groups. This makes sin an awkward topic of conversation. When it does come up in anything other than a theoretical context (gasp!) we tend to talk hesitantly, being careful to only use vague, safe terms. "Yes, I struggle sometimes," we confess to each other, while fidgeting with our Styrofoam coffee cups and staring at our shiny church shoes.

Then there's the fact that our culture finds the mere concept of sin laughable. Want to destroy your social life? Just bring up the topic of sin a time or two. Add all that up and you have a pretty good idea of why frank talk about this sin thing is so rare these days. Let alone a whole *book* on the subject.

But perhaps that's a good thing. Maybe books about sin should be rare.

The thing is, if sin is defined as operating outside of the will of God, then we shouldn't sit and read about sin, we should sit and read about the glory of God's will!

Our strategy should be to spend our time contemplating the beauty and simplicity and clarity of his commands, not contemplating how bad it is to disobey those commands.

The bold rallying cry of the gospel is never *Avoid Sin*. It has always been *Embrace Life!*

I have come that you might have life, and have it abundantly, Jesus said. Jesus has always been lavishly generous. And his gospel has always been more an invitation than a warning. What's our best strategy for remaining in his will? Simply, be enamored of his will. We should just open up a copy of the Gospels, sit at his feet, and listen to the splendor he calls us into. For the most part that will serve us much better than reading this little book you're holding now.

So why read this book at all? Why spend time and energy considering the realities of this distasteful, embarrassing thing called *sin*?

Because Jesus did.

It turns out Jesus was quite serious about sin. He taught specifically about sin and the nature of sin from time to time. The last year of my life has been marked by a bone-jarring collision with some of those teachings. It turns out that sometimes when Jesus taught about sin he got graphic, and passionate, and utterly sober.

And it turns out that the more I hear what Jesus has to say about sin, the more I have to admit that, deep within, I just plain don't agree with him. His odd opinions of sin just don't match up too well with my own sensible opinions.

So I've argued with him, wrestling with his teachings. And, slowly but clearly, his words have begun to reveal some deep-rooted lies inside of me. I'm beginning to see how I've been suckered by the enemy and seduced by my neighbors into believing all kinds of bald-faced lies about sin. Lies that directly contradict what Jesus himself taught so clearly. Smooth lies that steadily smother me and rob me of beauty.

The hard but welcome truth is that our world is way off when it comes to understanding sin. And it's getting to us. I know it has already gotten to me.

Thus this little book on sin.

Because if Jesus really came to grant us all clarity and understanding, to forever unmask the lies of the enemy, then I should listen to him. Even when it comes to his strange teachings about sin.

This simple study in the Gospels is a theological correction, then. It's a personal attempt to repent of my own views of sin and grab tightly onto the words of Jesus. It's a celebration of what Jesus' unfashionable truth can mean for us in our everyday lives.

And it's a short read all in all. So let's gather up our courage, pull up a seat next to Jesus, and talk of sin. It might not be comfortable. But as is always the case when submitting to our dear Jesus, it should prove to be a beautiful thing.

BOOK ONE

Why
Smell
Sin?

In which we discover

how Jesus approached

this uncomfortable topic.

DARKENING SOCK

It was a Sunday Morning.

I loved Sunday Mornings:
>   *my familiar pew,*
>   *my favorite hymn,*
>   *pastor's mildly entertaining 3rd point,*
>   *and the unmistakable, unique sound of . . .*
>   *sawing?*

Quite clear (from the pew behind, it seemed)
the tight rasp and rough grind of a saw.

There in church. On a Sunday Morning.

I turned to look, and my eyes grew.

A middle aged man with a receding hairline
bending far over, reaching toward the floor in front of him.

I looked closer, and my eyes grew.

He was working awkwardly
at his right ankle
with a red-handled, silver-toothed hack saw.
The cotton of his right tan dress sock
began to shred
and mingled with the flesh of his right ankle.
>   *Dark blood pulsed out*
>   *slowly darkening his sock and*
>   *spilling,*
>   *thickly,*
onto the gray all-purpose sanctuary carpet.

"Are you all right?" he asked
(quite sincere)
looking up at me and my gagging face.

1

But I Like My Eyeballs

If your right eye causes you to sin, tear it out and throw it away.

MATTHEW 5:29 NRSV

To be honest, I've never actually seen anyone saw off a foot. Their own foot, that is.

I've heard stories, of course. The stories all seem to be set in the deep woods. Someone gets trapped by a tree or tractor or some such heavy thing, and their only escape is to gnaw or hack vigorously at an ankle and then crawl about the wilderness looking for help.

There are variations: sometimes it's an arm caught under a fallen tree, sometimes a leg under a truck. But in all the stories it seems this sawing or gnawing off of feet or arms is meant to happen in the backwoods. Not a Broadway and Main kind of thing. Chopping off your hand while waiting at the counter at McDonald's, for example, just would not do. It's only for extreme cases where dark and heavy things are involved and there's no cell phone in sight.

If we experienced this little Darkening Sock encounter some Sunday for ourselves, we would most certainly be disturbed. Shocked even. Nauseated maybe. Sawing at tender skin and stubborn bone right there in church? Right in the pew behind you?

Maybe you're thinking there's something indecent about even *writing down* such images. Perhaps you think less of me as a writer for invoking this gore right here at the beginning of a book that's supposed to be about decent things like theology and God and religion.

Only problem: That's Jesus' gory image, not mine. Check it out. It's our Lord's very own. And there's nothing comforting about it.

So, let's just be painfully honest right from the get-go. Jesus had weird ideas about sin.

SIN IS *HOW* SERIOUS?

Consider. It was Jesus who looked into the weathered eyes of several strong, bearded fishermen and said with a straight face,

> If your right eye causes you to sin, tear it out and throw it away; it is better for you to lose one of your members than for your whole body to be thrown into hell. And if your right hand causes you to sin, cut it off and throw it away; it is better for you to lose one of your members than for your whole body to go into hell. (Matthew 5:29-30 NRSV)

Now, most of us have been taught to dismiss this teaching because "Jesus didn't literally mean we should pluck out our eyes." Instead of bristling at this teaching, we calmly lay it aside.

"Jesus was just using *hyperbole* here. He didn't really mean what he said." Ah, hyperbole, what a calm, intelligent-sounding word. So we smile and move on to other, more sensible teachings of Jesus that he clearly did mean to say.

But that isn't an explanation of this passage at all. We

are only assured of what the passage is *not* saying, which doesn't get us very far.

Just because Jesus may have not been "literal" in this teaching (that is, a correct application would not be to pluck out our eyes), that does not mean that he didn't intend to say precisely what he said here. Jesus is the ultimate communicator. He probably meant to say exactly what he said about eyes and hands and sin and such. In fact, we know that Jesus pronounced this teaching on more than one occasion. Later in the same Gospel we are told that Jesus said,

> If your hand or your foot causes you to sin, cut it off and throw it away; it is better for you to enter life maimed or lame than with two hands or two feet to be thrown into the eternal fire. And if your eye causes you to sin, pluck it out and throw it away; it is better for you to enter life with one eye than with two eyes to be thrown into the hell of fire. (Matthew 18:8-9)

So it turns out we didn't just catch Jesus on a bad metaphor day. Here he is, later in the same Gospel account, looking into the eyes of those same rough fishermen and making the same point. This should catch our theological attention.

In fact, we should be somewhat disturbed. After all, why did Jesus feel it necessary to give this seemingly unforgettable teaching more than once? Even if these two moments recorded by Matthew were the only two times Jesus ever taught this, why repeat himself even once? Both times Jesus is addressing the same disciples. And both times he uses these uncomfortable, unforgettable word pictures.

And by the way, why did he think it necessary to use such graphic imagery in the first place? Was he purposely trying to gross out his listeners? Or was gouging out one's eye a less grotesque metaphor in Jesus' day? (I don't think so.)

And why rehearse the gore over and over? He made his point with the eye. Why involve the hand? Why take the hacksaw to the foot too? Were the disciples so slow that he had to use this kind of bloody repetition just to get his point across?

My questions don't stop here, either, because this drastic approach to sin was regular for Jesus. Consider another graphic image of his:

> If any of you put a stumbling block before one of these little ones who believe in me, it would be better for you if a great millstone were fastened around your neck and you were drowned in the depth of the sea. (Matthew 18:6 NRSV)

Is anyone else noticing a theme here? Why does Jesus feel it so necessary to paint horrible word pictures when he's talking about sin?

Taking these vivid teachings seriously is what has plunged me into a deep wrestling match with Jesus. The more I look at them, the more they bother me. I try to dodge them as I have been taught to. *He's using hyperbole,* I murmur to myself. I try to tame them into some smooth theology, but they still bother me. The hair on these words just won't lie down all the way. Theological cowlicks galore!

I find genuine discomfort in his simple, graphic, repeating images. They haunt me. And perhaps that's precisely what Jesus intended.

So I've wrestled with them. And I think they won. Through these haunting images, Jesus has spoken loudly and all too clearly to my soul. The strong message that has emerged to pin me is a simple one: SIN IS SERIOUS.

Sin is serious. Jesus may not have been teaching us to pluck out our eyes literally, but he was definitely teaching us to take sin seriously. Very seriously. These images must have shocked and disturbed the disciples just as they do us. Their gore was not a mistake. It was a wake-up call. A "perspective check" that leaves us reeling today, just as it must have left his disciples every time he spoke these words to them.

We should choose to lose an eye rather than to sin. We should consider ourselves lucky to be drowned rather than to cause someone to sin. Wow.

Make no mistake about it, Jesus tells us with clarity through these haunting images, *sin is more serious than you might have guessed*.

A HOLE IN OUR THEOLOGY

Jesus is making claims here that violate my innate sense of what is important. My eyes, for example. Though Jesus might not literally be suggesting I maim myself by plucking out an eye, he most certainly is suggesting that avoiding sin is so important that even favorite, seemingly essential body parts pale in comparison.

Now I think avoiding sins is important. But I'm not sure it's *that* important! Which leaves me in a dilemma.

Either I am grossly overestimating how utterly terrible it would be to be drowned or I am woefully underestimating just how bad sin really is. It has to be one or

the other. I don't know about you, but to me being tied
with strong, binding ropes to a huge rock and getting
tossed into the sea just sounds bad. Really bad, terribly
bad (stop me if I'm overestimating just how bad it would
be)—horrendously, nightmarishly, horrifically bad! It
would be so bad to be drowned that it makes me start to
wonder if maybe I don't understand exactly how serious
sin really is.

You can see why I'm bothered, can't you? I'm bothered because I like my eyeballs. I do. And given these
teachings I see that I must have either an inflated sense of
the value of my eyes or a grossly deflated view of my sin.

Jesus' working assumptions about sin collide with
my own, and I am left considering the very real possibil-
ity that I believe lies about sin. Perhaps I have a gaping
hole in my theology.

Perhaps sin looks—even smells—different than I
have ever thought. Much different.

WEEPING ARCHER

The archer stood erect, his brown eyes riveted
    in front of him.

In one motion
his right hand pulled an arrow from the quiver on
his back and had it loaded
      with precision (and obvious strength)
        on the taut string.

He was all precision and purpose and concentration.

And then the arrow flew! And missed.

His handsome face tightened.
A slow tear flowed down his strong, brown face.

And he started to sway—slightly forward,
    slightly backward . . .
until he collapsed. And wept.
A dark, sad mud formed as he wept on the dry,
    dusty ground.

2

Smelling Sin

I will show you what it's like.
LUKE 6:47

In my everyday life I must admit that, given the choice, I'd really rather cause someone to sin (lie, maybe, or skip honoring the Sabbath some week) than be thrown into the cold, deep ocean with a millstone roughly tied to my skinny neck. I really would. Wouldn't you?

But admitting that fact is theologically awkward. It betrays that I disagree with Jesus. Which is not only embarrassing, but personally disturbing. After all, how can I be so far off on a basic truth like this? I read the Bible. I go to church. I'm a *serious* Christian, after all. How is it that I can still disagree with Jesus?

CHRISTENDOM AND MISSING THE MARK

Sin.

The Greek word used in the New Testament is *harmatia*. It literally means "to miss the mark." Now, that sounds pretty right to us. If righteousness is hitting the mark, then to miss that mark is to sin. Makes sense.

So, most of the time we Christians spend discussing *harmatia*, we're asking the question *What is the mark?*

or *What* is not *the mark?* It's really a question of defi-
nition: *What is sin?*

Now, this is a very important question. If sin is the act
of missing the mark, then it's pretty important to know
where exactly that mark is! What *is* the target? And (perhaps equally important) what's *outside* the target?

These important questions are the stomping
grounds for most of Christendom's talk and worry over
sin. We busy ourselves examining the edges of the target. Our communities and denominations spend great
time and energy deciding what's really too far out from
the target to be a "hit" anymore. And we personally
make mental lists of what we can and cannot do in
good conscience.

Sometimes it's easy to make the list. Murder, lying,
adultery, hitting people with sticks and stones. But sometimes it's not so easy. Divorce, euthanasia, speeding,
thinking about hitting people with sticks and stones?

Here Christendom is split. Sides are drawn, argu-
ments fly like daggers, and we debate the meaty issues of
the day with vigor. We've got this strong, innate desire to
answer that hugely important question: *What is sin?*

We need these debates. In this world of compromise,
blurred edges and an ever-shifting Post-It note morality,
we need to sit at Jesus' feet and hear what he has to say
about what is sin and what is not.

It is a very important question. But it's not the only
question to ask when it comes to sin.

JESUS AND MISSING THE MARK

Interestingly, Jesus spent his time differently than we do
when it came to talking about *harmatia*. For starters, we

rarely see Jesus expounding detailed lists of sins, as we are so quick to do.

But this doesn't mean he was silent on the topic of sin. Far from it. Jesus spent great time and energy talking about sin. And as it turns out, the lion's share of that teaching falls under two themes.

The first theme has to do with forgiveness. Interestingly, much of the time when Jesus mentioned the noun *sin* he was speaking of forgiveness. Find him using the noun, and you'll usually hear of the beautiful forgiveness of sins. Jesus told parable after parable of a shocking grace that was being made possible through him. And (though it enflamed the religious folks of the day) he often forgave people of their sins right there on the spot!

The second theme has to do with what it is like to sin. This theme emerges when we look at the times Jesus spoke of the verb, *the act* of sinning. These are the times he got graphic. His words were not the gentle, beautiful words of forgiveness but vivid, shocking words that commanded attention!

Find him using the verb, find him talking about the act of sinning, and you will find plucked eyes and heavy millstones and sawed-through ankles. You'll find all the surprising images we will take a look at in part two. Jesus drew attention to these serious images trying to show us just what it's like to sin.

It's a profound thing to consider. Jesus didn't spend all of his time passing on detailed lists of sins; instead, he also felt it important to paint pictures of what it's like to sin—and to speak of the sweet forgiveness of the sins themselves.

Now Christendom has done a pretty good job with

the first theme: Jesus' talk of the forgiveness of sins. And what a beautiful thing to have clarity about! More than anything we need to hear those grace-filled words about forgiveness that he has for the world and for us. We need to contemplate and celebrate the cross. We need to proclaim—loudly—the redemption for sins that Jesus has made possible for all who will come to him.

And we do. Praise God for all our talk and singing and writing about the immeasurable gift of salvation!

But what about the other theme Jesus spent so much time on? All of Jesus' teaching about what it's like to sin—we seem to have forgotten all about that. Shouldn't we heed this teaching as well and find out why Jesus spent so much time and energy painting so many vivid word pictures of the act of sinning?

It may be that we are more accustomed to discussing the question *What is sin?* But Jesus also posed this very different question: *What is it like to sin?*

THE NEED TO SMELL SIN

If our theological cry is *Define sin!* then Jesus' refrain is a resounding *Smell sin!*

Yes, *smell* it. If sinning is missing the target, Jesus spent all kinds of time and energy trying to get across to his followers not just what that target was, but what it was like to miss that target.

What's it *like* to miss the target? This is a question about feeling, a question that invokes senses and mood, not calculators and rulers. With this question Jesus invites us not just to scientifically define, categorize and list sins. He invites us to sniff—to find out the feel and taste and smell of sinning. To pay attention to the dirty details and subtle nuances and really understand the *feel* of sin.

But why? Why spend so much time on the smell and feel of missing the target? After all, does it really even matter what it's *like* to miss a target? Isn't it enough to just know we're not supposed to miss?

Well, consider the Weeping Archer. If, on your own, you were asked to imagine a man with a taut bow shooting at a target and missing, what would you imagine? In the moments following the miss, what's the mood, the *smell* of the moment?

Is he laughing? Is he frustrated? Do you see him being scolded by his archery teacher? Or is he weeping uncontrollably? All of these are possible moods of the missing; there are many ways that his missing of the mark could "smell."

If he's goofing around with some friends, his miss might be funny—hilarious, even! But if he's in a tournament and the team's pride and final standing are on the line, his miss might smell of shame and guilt. And what if the target isn't just a piece of paper on a hay bale but an apple balanced on someone's head? Ooh. *Then* missing could smell quite different. A whole new level of seriousness! And whose head *is* it, after all? His evil enemy's—or his wife's?

Weeping could follow the missing, but so could a ticker tape parade. Two very different smells indeed.

Doesn't it stand to reason that any sane archer should know what it's going to be like to miss before drawing back that sharp arrow and taking aim? Of course. What if he *thought* he was goofing around, but in reality it was the finals of the tournament? What if he thought the ap-

ple was balanced on his archenemy's head, but alas, it
was his true love under that small apple who caught his
errant arrow? Ah, weeping archer.

Knowing the smell of potentially missing the mark
could make all the difference in the world for him. And
being deceived about the smell of missing could prove
horrendous in his life.

Or imagine you come across a jar of brown liquid in
your fridge with a note taped to it saying, "DON'T
DRINK!" What would it be like to "miss the mark" set
down in that emphatic note and drink it anyway? And
does it really matter what it would be like?

Well, if it turns out to be some refreshing sun tea
made by your roommate (who's out of town for two
weeks anyway), then disobeying the note was no big
deal. You got a refreshing taste of "forbidden" tea. You
can replace it before the roommate gets back. What was
it like to disobey the note? It was cool!

But what if that jar turns out to be full of gasoline that
your dad drained from the malfunctioning chain saw
and for some reason (it's your dad, after all) decided to
keep in the fridge? Well, if that's the situation, then the
mood or smell of disobeying that note's warning is very
different! It could actually kill you.

What's it like to miss that mark? It's cool, or it kills
you. Hmmm. Kind of makes you want to know what it
would be like to miss before deciding whether or not to
chug away, doesn't it? Knowing the true smell might affect how you feel about that note taped to the jar. And it
might even determine what you choose to do.

And as with sharp arrows and forbidden liquids, so
it is with sin.

Sinning is missing the mark, to be sure. But when I give into temptation and I sin, am I teased as *naughty,* yelled at as an *idiot* or pronounced *dead?* Perhaps Jesus knew that my careful defining of the target would ultimately make a difference only if I truly understood what it would be like to miss it.

Perhaps Jesus sees that, in the end, all of our detailed lists will do us little good if we don't ask this question of smell. Maybe that's precisely why he taught so extensively on the smell of sin (and why the enemy has tried so tirelessly to deceive us about the same).

Jesus gave us pictures and images, not just lists and definitions. Let's not ignore him. Let's ask the theological question Jesus himself felt was so important.

What *is* the smell of sin?

BOOK TWO

Blowing Our Theological Noses

In which we get honest about how we usually view sin.

AFTERNOON SNACK

A glass of milk
　　　white and cold and ready to do the body good
is forgotten

Forgotten.

Busy kitchen, crowded Christmastime counter with bows
and wrapping paper and keys and
forgotten milk.
Milk festering. Hardening.
Clumping in anger.

The poor boy strolled (unnoticed) into the kitchen
　　　with a cold
　　　　　and a stuffed-up nose
　　　　　　　(innocent eyes)

and an afternoon snack
of milk chunks.

3

Santa Claus

You have heard it said . . . but I say to you . . .
MATTHEW 5:21-22

What is the smell of sin?

Well, before we dive into what Jesus says sin smells like, it is important to first clear our noses of other "scents" of sin we might have picked up over the years. We aren't starting with a clean slate here. Our theological noses are probably crowded with false smells, with very clear beliefs about sinning that have *not* come from Jesus.

Many have come from the utterly confused world around us. And a few, perhaps, from the enemy himself.

So let's bravely name and honestly try to get rid of some of these false smells before approaching what Jesus himself has to say about the true smell of sin.

SANTA CLAUS?

We've said that sin is "missing the mark." But let's face it: our society as a whole does not believe that there is a "mark to shoot for." Today's Western culture says there is no one right way to live.

Our smiling neighbors mostly just shrug and conclude there is nothing inherent in creation that would insist that there is a "mark." *Like, there's this feeling within all of us that says that we're all just on a ride! Do what you want. Dance, run, walk, sit, spit . . . whatever! No choice is inherently "better" or "worse" than any other. Sin? How medieval!*

What does our culture think of sin? This is a little like asking what people in our culture think of unicorns. Most know that unicorns are a myth. So the debate is: is it a cute myth or a silly myth or a destructive one? Sin really has joined the ranks of Santa Claus and the Easter Bunny in our culture: something that you once believed in as a child but have since grown out of.

Our culture loves to "enlighten" us and free us from these repressive old-fashioned myths. It's a little like being the kid whose progressive parents let him in on the secret early in life—"Sorry, there is no Santa Claus, Georgie. We respect you too much to lie to you anymore."

Enlightened early in life, Georgie is the child who smugly shakes his head while he listens to his deceived classmates talk excitedly of Santa, or who becomes the cruel bearer of truth, choosing weak classmates whose false hopes need some crushing: "Hey Sally—there is no Santa Claus! Just ask your parents!"

Poor Sally. She tries to hold back her tears while flustering brave statements about never having believed any of that stuff anyway.

In the same way, by the time folks grow up and learn a thing or two, they pick up the view that sin is a phantom—a myth made up and perpetuated by parents who are either still sadly deceived or, more likely, just looking for a way to control their kids.

So, what does sin smell like to most of our neighbors? Nothing. Air.

Smells like Santa Claus.

Sin has joined the ranks of Santa Claus and cupids and unicorns in the Playland of Mythdom. Except sin doesn't have a SuperMyth costume. Not easily recognizable and parodied, sin is slipping to the back corners of Mythdom. Even Satan—who set up shop next to Santa and the Tooth Fairy long before sin—remains popular and parodied. With his red horns, pointed tail and red SuperMyth cape, Satan gets all kinds of gigs! He's really popular around Halloween. But not sin.

Sin is forgotten. Destined to an obscure life at the back of our childhood memories. Santa Claus has even been seen bullying sin around from time to time. Always easy to pick on the little guy.

UNREAL?

Sin has no smell. No flesh, no shape, no mass or heft or sound. Makes no impressions at all.

Nothing.

Though the pages of the Bible tell us with wide-eyed clarity that sin is real, the air we breathe, the streets we walk and the siren voices we're bombarded with every day tell us otherwise: Sin is a myth.

Sin is a *myth?* That's a lie that would get laughed out of the room in many cultures and countries on our planet. "Of course sin exists! Just look around! There's right, and there's wrong. And wrong gets punished." But there's something about our softly cushioned, air-conditioned bubbles of academia and suburbia that gives this ridiculous lie room to strut. It holds its head high, its shoulders wide.

"Sin is a myth, just like Santa Claus." Scripture re-

nounces that idea for the lie it is. Reality mocks it. But
the happy smell of Santa Claus wafts past our theological noses on a regular basis. And we subconsciously
breathe this lie into our souls all day long like so much
spiritual laughing gas. We'd never say we really believed it, but it bleeds into our minds and our theology,
quietly and persistently, day by day.

AFTERNOON SNACK
(take two)

Forgotten milk
sits guarded.

"Young man! Don't you even get near that glass of milk!"

His young body shrugs defensively.
But his eyes grow wide, and peer.
And long.

"Young man! Stop staring! That milk is so bad for you!
It's rotten!"

No shrug this time.
Just seemingly averted eyes.
And a growing longing.

And an afternoon snack
of milk chunks.

4

Chalk Dust

> But [the older son] answered his father,
> "Listen! For all these years I have been
> working like a slave for you, and I have
> never disobeyed your command."
>
> LUKE 15:29 NRSV

We Christians are in on this huge secret: Sin exists! Both in our theology (most of the time) and in our hearts (some of the time) we know that sin is not a myth.

For many of us sin doesn't smell as much like Santa Claus as it does a classroom.

A grade-school classroom. You know the smells: freshly-cleaned linoleum floors, chalk dust, and (when you're old enough) that faint smell of formaldehyde wafting in from the biology lab. Straight rows of predictable desks. A rectangular chalkboard up front. And a bank of bright, inviting windows on one side.

And most of all, you know *She's* always somewhere in the room. *The Teacher*. Sometimes she sits on her throne behind her impressive Wooden Desk, eyeing the class. From up there she can take in the whole classroom without even having to turn her head. No blind spots to speak of. She knows all. She sees all. She is . . . The Teacher!

The Teacher had the authority to set the rules before you ever came into the classroom. Looming over the chalkboard as an ever-present reminder is a laminated poster listing "The Rules." And you've always got that nagging feeling that she could change any of those rules without notice. Because, well, she is The Teacher, after all.

As ominous as her level-gazed perch behind her Desk can be, it is nothing compared to The Stroll. Sure, it seems innocent enough—she is walking casually between the tight rows of desks, hands clasped behind her back—but looks can be deceiving!

When she's behind her Desk, you know where she is. But on The Stroll? She could be coming up the right side, or circling around the left. And you know you aren't supposed to look around to find out. "No wandering eyes!" She could be clear across the room looking out the window or, for all you know, standing right behind you staring at your sweaty, shaking hand as it tries to correctly copy the spelling words.

And if you *do* transgress one of the Laminated Rules and She finds out (which she always does!), you will be punished. Punished. You are *Naughty*. And The Teacher is not happy.

THE LIST LASTS

Sin smells like that. Like a childhood classroom. Fear. A desire to not be caught. And, especially as time goes by, a nagging sense that the rules are somewhat arbitrary. (Which is somewhat disconcerting, but what can you do? The List of Rules is laminated, after all, and was hung grandly above the chalkboard years before you ever got into the classroom!)

In many of us that fear eventually dulls and is replaced by a secret feeling of annoyance. Over the years we start to figure out that almost all of the forbidden actions listed among the Laminated Rules are the more fun things in life. No talking. No paper airplanes. Running, passing notes, making fart noises, playing with scissors . . . all the good things in the classroom are forbidden!

And to top it all off, most of the students in the class are doing those very things and seeming to have a great time of it! In fact, when we stop to look around we notice that we Christians are the only ones who are still in our seats, let alone the only ones still copying the spelling words!

And the rest of the folks in class don't mind pointing and laughing at us and our neat desks and completed assignments and patiently raised hands! I know it's nearly unthinkable, but they . . . well, they don't even ask for the bathroom pass anymore. They do as they please in this loose world of ours.

But the Laminated List still hangs. And The Teacher—she may not get any respect from most in the class, but she's still there.

She's still there. But it sure doesn't seem like she's doing much Punishing. And it makes me gaze at the Laminated Rules with more cynicism than fear these days. *Stupid poster!* I think sometimes. But I don't say it out loud. Not while I'm in the classroom, anyway.

I know I'm supposed to really love the list (it's a *gift* from the teacher to me) and really hate what's forbidden (it *is* quite dangerous to run with scissors). But in day-to-day practice I just don't feel that love or that hatred.

Lately I've begun bending some of the sillier rules.

No one notices, of course. I'm actually fitting in more than ever. I'm sure the teacher will understand, if she notices.

And that's it. That's what sin smells like. None of us would officially sign off on a theology of sin that sounded like that, of course. We're far too dutiful and polite. But for some of us, our hearts signed off on it long ago.

We still struggle to obey. We still long to be obedient. And disciplined. We want to please The Teacher, of course. But that is how sin feels to us. That's what it's *like*.

And although many of us debate vigorously what, exactly, is on that infamous Laminated List, we all agree that it does *feel* like a list. A list of rules in the classroom of life. Written by The Teacher. And though the classroom has gone wild and students are even seen spitting at The Teacher, we still try to remember to capitalize the T's, and we long to obey.

Now, we know that missing the mark can't really smell like a classroom. That would fly in the face of almost everything about God's relationship with us that is revealed in Scripture. The idea of God being some anonymous teacher who stands over us waiting for us to screw up violates so many beautiful truths about our relationship with God. It demeans and perverts what God does for us and offers us. It belittles and cheapens the true work of Jesus' Spirit inside of us.

But when we're honest, some of us must admit that the smell of a classroom sure has found its way into our theological noses.

AFTERNOON SNACK
(take three)

Forgotten milk . . .
              Found!

Found and celebrated!
Celebrated and spotlighted and interviewed and admired
      and photographed and
loved and sung about—oh, so beautifully!

Ah, forgotten milk!
Those subtle mixes of white and off-white!
This complex struggle between liquid and solid!
That time of prude spurning (quietly endured) forever over!

Oh, glass of complexity.
Oh, evolution of milk.

Oh, afternoon snack
of milk chunks.

5

Popcorn

> *But the serpent said to the woman,*
> *"You will not die; for God knows that*
> *when you eat of [the fruit] your eyes*
> *will be opened, and you will be like*
> *God, knowing good and evil."*
>
> GENESIS 3:4-5

For others, sin doesn't smell as much like a myth or a classroom as it does a rip-roaring carnival.

A wild, exciting, brightly lit carnival on a warm Friday night. The smell of fresh popcorn, sweet pink cotton candy and warm spilled beer seeping into the carpet of stomped-down green grass between the thrilling rides and intriguing tents. Ahh, the smells of a carnival!

What's it like to sin? It's fun. Tremendous fun! Like a carnival!

Now we know we're not supposed to go to that fun carnival because Jesus' *Land o' Boredom and Righteousness* (which is set up on the other side of town) might lose some business. But just look at the rides! Look at the huge crowds of laughing people! Just take a whiff of that popcorn!

The way of God just seems so stuffy and boring and . . . right. Yes, it's *right*, of course. But I'm sure Jesus will understand; he was human, after all. He knows how absolutely delicious the carnival looks to us. And if he really expected us to stay 24-7 in his *Land o' Boredom and Righteousness,* he would have thought up some better rides than organ playing and Bible reading.

Now, again, many of us would never *say* we thought sin was like a carnival. Perhaps we even blush to read it expressed so frankly. But this small lie is insidious; it inhabits the very air we breathe! It is shouted all around us and then it sets up home inside of us. And, like leaven in dough, it can eventually have its way with our hearts.

Sin is fun, we hear. It's a small lie. Only three words. None of them over three letters. But it's a powerful lie. *Sin is fun.* We breathe it in . . . and doubt rises in our hearts. We try to remain dutiful, but this lie sows seeds of rebellion and dissatisfaction within us. They eat away at our faith and joy like a herd of spiritual termites. God starts to seem the kill-joy and the enemy starts to seem so life-giving and fun.

Sin is fun. Righteousness is boring. These days the noses of our souls grow mighty confused. The smell of hot buttered popcorn is impossible to ignore.

It almost goes without saying that all of this nonsense is wretchedly false through and through. Scripture shows this little lie for the utter perversion it is. God must groan over the places in our hearts where this lie has pitched its tent and begun to settle in. And Satan, our enemy, must snicker to himself that we've swallowed such a big, fetid lie.

But there the smell is, living inside our theological noses.

THE DANGER OF FALSE SMELLS

There are other false smells, of course.

For example, some feel that sin smells like fresh air—like release from the oppressive, male-dominated church institution and all the weights it has thrust upon humankind. Sin is freedom and self-expression ("Go ahead, have some fun!")—a deep, refreshing breath for our souls.

But whatever the false smells inside each of us—whether Santa Claus or popcorn or a little of both—it's important that we name them. It's not enough to just strive to be orthodox in our defining of sins. We can have the most biblical list of sins around, we can define "missing the mark" with more precision than anyone, and yet if we believe false things about what it's like to miss that mark, we're in trouble.

We're in trouble because over time these false smells hold sway over our hearts. They affect our posture and energy and our attitude toward righteousness. If we feel inside that sin really is like being naughty in a classroom or like having fun in a forbidden amusement park, that will necessarily affect our actions.

Perhaps we'll start to only vaguely "feel sorry" when we sin. We'll utter some tepid prayer out of habit, but it'll feel more like a mantra than something deep and real happening inside us. Jesus' comments such as "he who is forgiven much, loves much" will seem enigmatic and obscure. We might even start to feel awkward singing "Amazing Grace." That phrase "a wretch like me" seems to be overstating matters a bit.

And, sadly but inevitably, a few of our sins will become favorites. We may "repent" of them. We may repent hundreds of times a year! Sure, these favorite sins are forbidden, we know, just like running with scissors and throwing spit wads. But it doesn't seem to make a huge difference to us. We just keep on with our favorite sins. Despite our best intentions we sin often and with few second thoughts.

These false smells certainly could lead us into real trouble. We might even find ourselves with gaping holes in our theology!

The thing is, these false smells just don't match up with what Jesus teaches. If sin is really like Santa Claus and unicorns, then Jesus' passionate words about plucking out our eyes and being drowned by millstones are ludicrous.

If sin is really as frivolous as the joy of an amusement park, then Jesus' sober posture toward sin is simply silly.

If sin smells like disobeying random rules in a strict classroom, then Jesus' passionate images about sin are just a waste of time.

These seemingly benign false smells are mighty dangerous. We think they are the smell of sin. Makes me wonder what Jesus thought sin really smelled like. If not like a myth, a list of classroom rules, or a fun ride . . . then what? What is the true smell of sin?

BOOK THREE

The
Smell
of Sin

In which we gaze on

the unforgettable images

Jesus painted of sin.

BEING ONE

After the initial shock,
the panic of seeing them eating together
                so intimate
at that Italian Restaurant.

After the bitter fighting
and smashing all the family pictures and ripping
        nearly everything in his closet.

After the shameful letter to the family and the
        glaring looks in court
and the large settlement and the 2 weeks on Cozumel.

After the very old wine and the very young men
        and the new car
and the remodel and the name change and
        the slightly strained laughter . . .

That one moment remains.
Seeing his hand holding hers.

6

Spitting on Mom

> Those who love me will keep my word,
> and my Father will love them, and we
> will come to them and make our home
> with them.
>
> JOHN 14:23 NRSV

> The younger son said to his father,
> "Give me my share of the property that
> falls to me." Not many days later
> this son just left.
>
> LUKE 15:12-13

Jesus says all sin takes place in a home.

What pictures does he paint to give us a clear sense of what it's like to miss the mark? Jesus tells us to imagine not a cold, rigid classroom but a warm family home.

We are to picture not a classroom with desks and blackboards but a familiar kitchen with hot food and warm, knowing smiles. A place of innocent pranks and easy laughter. A home.

Jesus says that if I follow him he smiles and calls me kin. I'm family. *And looking around on those who sat about him, he said, "Whoever does the will of God is my brother, and sister, and mother"* (Mark 3:34-35).

Anyone who follows Jesus is adopted into his fam-

ily. We actually become children of God, people born
of God (John 1:12-13). And that's not just a metaphor,
that's a spiritual reality.

Jesus said plainly that he will come and make a home
together with us. He patiently melts away our serious, stiff
theology by calmly telling us that we have a loving father.
The best father ever! That's what it's like, Jesus says.

> There was this father who had two sons. One day he sent
> them out to work the land with him. (Matthew 21:28-32)

> There was a father who had two sons, a younger son and
> an older son. One day the younger son went up to his fa-
> ther. (Luke 15:11-12)

> Pray like this, "Our . . ." (Matthew 6:9)

Multiple times Jesus began explaining a theological
truth by first painting a picture of a family—a kid with a
loving parent. You want to understand about God, about
sin, about deep spiritual realities? Well, imagine a dad
and his kids at home together. This is the context for understanding sin.

Want to know the smell of sin? Jesus says we should
try to imagine a smooth-skinned Jewish son telling his
bearded father to hand over his inheritance (Luke
15:11-32). This in a time when a son was literally identified by who his father was. (For example, Jesus' "last
name" was *bar Joseph*. Literally, Jesus *the son of Joseph*.) This in a time where land, family and survival
were inextricably and joyfully tied together.

Imagine! Jesus whispered, *This son went up to his loving father and said, "Give me my share—I'm leaving!"*

The Jewish men in Jesus' crowd must have cringed.
For a son to do such a thing was unthinkable. *Then his*

father handed it over! And . . . the son left! Now the listeners felt nauseated. With clenched fists they tried to imagine what they would do with such a son!

That's what sin smells like.

Another time, Jesus told another crowd to *imagine a father, with two sons* (Matthew 21:28-32). *The father asked them in the morning to go into the fields to work, as usual. One son said "No way!" but, of course, went and worked the land that day.* Again a cringing audience. How could a son speak to his father like that!

But the second . . . Here the crowd waits to hear of the hero, the good, polite, loving son. *The second says "Of course, my father! I will go work the land!"*

The crowd smiles and nods. Jesus prepares the ending of the story.

But he doesn't! He never goes out to work the land that day. Gasps. Shocked looks. The indignity, the dishonor, the shame!

"What an insult!" the Jewish men sputter as they shake their bearded heads in disgust. Inside, they are quietly thankful that their sons would never do such a thing.

That's what it smells like, Jesus says. The *mark?* A loving family. Missing the mark? Insult and rebellion against a loving, gentle parent.

A HOT BREAKFAST

Just imagine you're back at home with your parents. You've slept in and are aroused from your grogginess by the rich smells of bacon and coffee. You smile and roll out of bed.

Rounding the corner into the kitchen you see an intense spread on the table—all your favorites! A pile of steaming bacon on a platter in the middle, a huge carafe of orange juice (looks fresh-squeezed!), cheddar cheese thickly seeping out of the four-egg omelet on your plate. You smile and sigh.

Your family around the table is chatting as only family can. They smile as you enter the room. Then you see her. She straightens up in front of the open oven, and as she turns you see her familiar, faded-lilac apron and a tray of fresh cinnamon rolls that fills the room with the hope of a good day. She walks over with a quick smile and a wink and sets the tray right next to your place at the table. A gentle "Good morning, honey" invites you to take your seat with the family.

Your youngest sister starts to giggle—just because! Because it's a good morning and she's at home with her family. You walk up to your lovely mom—and spit directly in her face.

That's what it's like, Jesus says.

Afterward, the room would be dead silent, of course. Mom would quickly close both eyes, and the spit would drip slowly down her shocked, hurt face. She would most likely raise her apron, more to hide her face than to clean it.

That's what sin smells like.

Sin always takes place in a home. Sin is a revolt against a loving parent. No disappointed teacher, rather a hurt father. An insulted mother. Not stern looks so much as quiet, deep weeping.

God made this clear as he reasoned with sinful Israel through his prophets. "You are my bride," he would say, "and I am your loving husband. When you sin you are adulterous. You are playing the harlot." God does not glare at us in our sin. Rather, his face has the look of a betrayed husband (Hosea 1:2).

When we lie to a friend, we aren't getting away with a silly *naughty-naughty*. We're not just pulling the wool over the teacher's eyes. We're spitting in the face of our father. That's what Jesus says it's like.

When I ignore the Sabbath, I'm not just forgetting some ancient, random rule about work and rest. I am turning my back on my father. It's like I'm flipping off the only constant, forgiving loved one that I have.

When I sin I'm tempted to believe that I'm just frustrating a tall, impersonal teacher. That's easier to believe than what Jesus says. It's easy to frustrate a teacher. It's painful to insult a parent. The stakes are much higher, the implications much deeper.

Consider Peter. A strong, able, opinionated man. A doer, proactive in every way. Why is it that this same Peter is reduced to tears after betraying Jesus? Why does this bearded fisherman weep? And why is his weeping described as *bitter* (Matthew 26:75)?

Not because he was afraid of punishment, to be sure. Not because he was embarrassed at having been proven wrong in his earlier argument with Jesus about whether or not he would ever forsake Jesus.

He wept for the simple reason that Jesus was so dear to him. It was *his* Jesus he had betrayed. Peter wasn't worried about being grounded or stuck in the corner—these were not the tears of a boy sent to the principal's office. He had betrayed his sweet Jesus.

When I'm tempted to sin I'm never considering whether or not to be *naughty*. I'm contemplating insulting my dear Father.

And what was Jesus' question when he was reunited with Peter (John 21:15-17)? "Do you love me?"

Not a biting "Are you going to screw up again?" Or even a frustrated "Don't you have the list down yet?" But a gentle, to-the-point "Do you love me?"

God is not angry at our sin so much as he is hurt and betrayed. His teeth may grind from time to time. But mostly he cries.

This is the smell of sin, according to Jesus.

ONE CAR GARAGE

She slid in behind the wheel   with anger,
her teeth clenched, her eyes serious—aimed straight ahead.

With thin young fingers she turned the key
and began to rev the engine over and over   and over,
her eyes straight ahead,
      her fingers tight
              around the steering wheel.
The engine growled   and roared
              and spat
in chorus with her soul.

And the car went nowhere.

Eventually her foot faltered and slipped off the gas pedal.
Eventually her heavy head slumped, lifeless,
      onto the black vinyl steering wheel.
And (for a moment) young tears dropped easily
      from her closed eyes
onto the hard black plastic cruise control buttons.

7

Revolt of the Branches

> *If you keep my commandments, you will abide in my love.*
>
> JOHN 15:10 NRSV

> *If a man does not abide in me, he withers.*
>
> JOHN 15:6

Sin is suicide.

Jesus was not vague on this point. When we sin, God does not shake a finger with a stiff "How dare you!" He shrugs slowly in confusion, and with a sad voice asks, "Why *would* you?"

He asks this with a sad voice because sin is suicide. Spiritual suicide.

To be in the will of God, to hit the mark, is to be fed, to find life. That is the clear refrain of the Gospels. Jesus is life to us. He is bread and calls to a hungry, starving people, offering himself. He is water and calls to a thirsty woman, offering himself.

I am the life, he assures his followers (John 14:6). *Just remain in me, abide in me and you will live* (John 15:4).

Hitting the mark is to be plugged into the only source of life and nourishment. So, to miss the mark? To sin is to choke yourself. To commit suicide. It doesn't matter how slowly or quickly—suicide is suicide.

Jesus asks us to imagine a renegade branch that decides it wants to abandon the vine with its trunk and deep roots. Silly brown branch. Feeling strong, it marches off in its own direction. The other branches notice its strut and feel swayed.

Who says we have to stay here with the vine? the branches begin to wonder. "How old-fashioned and limiting!" one brave branch sneers loudly. And before you know it a genuine Revolt of the Branches has begun!

Their twig legs stretch and their eyes grow wide in their newfound freedom. No more "vine-sitting," they say! The word *vine* is spat out with disgust. This is the twenty-first century, by golly! Twigs are meant to roam where their hearts dictate!

Now what do we make of these rebelling branches? *Naughty*? No, that word doesn't quite seem appropriate. *Foolish* gets much closer. *Idiotic* perhaps?

They're destroying themselves! It doesn't matter what inspiring spin they put on it, this haughty independence cannot be good for them. No matter where they march, they're dying. There are certain physical and botanical laws that they just cannot run from. As sure as the sun comes up in the early morning, they will shrivel up and die. No question.

Well, that's what Jesus said sin is like. To sin is to turn one's head from life. To spurn the source of nourishment and go in one's own direction. And it will, he assured his disciples in simple words, end in spiritual suicide.

THE PICNIC

Imagine a young child sitting near the beach with her

parents. There's a great picnic spread before her—a wonderfully thick checkered blanket on the grass simply covered with goodies! Watermelon, of course. And sharp cheddar cheese with crackers, and a bowl of steaming corn on the cob. Deviled eggs and chocolate cookies and dill pickles, and a clear glass pitcher full of cold lemonade and clinking chunks of ice.

It's a good day.

The sun is overhead and the breeze is blowing slightly, just enough to keep the flies away. But the daughter? The little girl sitting on the grass next to the blanket? Well, she's eating, that's for sure. But she's eating dirt-covered *rocks.*

Yes, rocks. As sure as the grass is green and the sun warms the air, she's picking up pebbles and stones from the ground around her . . . and eating them! Her teeth are beginning to chip and crack in places. And there's blood beginning to drip out of her tiny mouth. But she's forcing a smile.

Of course, her parents try desperately to stop her! But she's a determined little girl. And the longer she goes without real food, the more desperate she gets. She's grabbing fistfuls now. Grass, rocks, dirt, twigs all together being shoved into her young mouth.

And her parents weep beside her. The sad sight of her frenzy next to the wonderful food they've prepared is too much. The blood from her mouth is dripping onto her yellow sundress. And her hands are beginning to shake. The parents plead desperately through flowing tears.

"Honey, those aren't good for you! You're breaking your teeth, honey. Look!" They try not to break down.

"Look at the yummy watermelon on the blanket; won't you eat that?" Their words are tender.

"*Your* blanket!" her voice is high and harsh. "I'm through being stifled by your blanket!"

"But . . ." The parents start up in disbelief.

"Get out of my face!" Her voice doesn't seem so young anymore. Tiny drops of blood splatter when she talks.

This little girl's parents aren't shaking fingers. They aren't dreaming up a punishment. They are weeping. For they know the blanket—and they know what rocks and grass do to a young body. They won't force-feed her cheese and watermelon. They weep because they know their daughter is slowly killing herself.

That's the smell of sin, according to Jesus.

I am the true vine. (John 15:1 NRSV)

I am the true bread, come down from heaven. (John 6:41)

All other vines and bread? They are false. They are rocks and grass and dirt.

And the proud branches bravely march away from the vine. They march into independence and exploration and death.

For what can a branch do apart from the vine? Jesus asked his disciples, perhaps with a parent's tears in his eyes. What can a branch do apart from the vine?

Nothing, he assured his followers, looking into their eyes. Nothing (John 15:5).

To do our father's will is to abide in the vine. To miss the mark? Well this, this is the slow death.

This absurd, brave march into starvation—that's what sin smells like. The stench of death. The tang of corpses. All within reach of a splendid feast, of a nourishing vine.

This is the smell of sin.

Jesus assured his followers over and over that his kingdom was like a huge feast. A wedding banquet. "Why would anyone," he wondered, "not come to the feast?" He knew the answer, of course. Excuses of land and cattle and wives. The stuff of life (Luke 14:16-24).

You see, the call to worship God and to have no other idols isn't some old-fashioned folk belief that (even though it's still on the laminated List of Rules) has simply outlived its time. Jesus says that if we hold anything more dearly than we hold him, we are cutting ourselves off from true life. The young man who idolizes his girlfriend and orbits his life around her is not merely "getting carried away." His idolizing of her is not just silly and romantic. He's choking himself.

IT'S DEADLY

To lie, to gossip, to show partiality, to think resentful thoughts toward someone, is to die. It's to grab hold of your own neck with both hands and squeeze. No wonder Jesus was so adamant: lose *a hand* or let that hand choke you and lose your *life*. To Jesus it seemed an easy decision.

How often, while giving in to temptation, do we feel this spiritual choking? How often while living in unrepentant sin do we feel a spiritual slowness, an aching within us that our indulgent pleasures just can't seem to cover up?

Consider my friend who collapsed beside me one night in a snowdrift. Through anguished tears he confessed a decade-long sin. He was in great misery. Through all the tears, though, there was the undeniable sense that his soul was taking a deep, long breath. It was as if he had been drowning or smothering for all those years and was just now able to come up for some spiritual air.

Confession is not a choking thing. It is breathing for the first time. Sin, itself, is what chokes.

As with Raskonikov in Dostoyevsky's *Crime and Punishment*, the unrepented sin eats away at mind, soul and—yes—even body. It is suicide. No wonder Jesus was so clear on this point.

When I'm considering whether or not to sin, I'm not considering whether or not to indulge an exciting fancy that might earn me the glare of the teacher and a seat in the corner. I'm not being tempted by a harmless night at a forbidden carnival. I'm considering whether or not to chew on spiritual rocks.

When I decide to give in to temptation, I'm not deciding to drink a forbidden but delicious drink. I'm deciding to down a glass of Clorox bleach. I'm taking poison. I'm not just naughty, I'm a fool.

This is the smell of sin, according to Jesus.

MERRY-GO-ROUNDS
DON'T ALWAYS STOP WHERE
THEY STARTED

the hard fiberglass, brightly painted horses
        slow
and slow from their wild gallop
        as the mechanical stampede hums
        and clicks   to a stop.

His silly young laughter
        settles
into quiet giggling
and a wide smile falls into a satisfied grin
        as the bright red carousel hums
        and clicks   to a stop.

He leans back and closes his eyes and
        feels
the wind on his grinning face
        as the wild circle of horses hums
        and clicks   to a stop.

And he lightly steps off
to greet
        a boiling sea of strange faces
        loud and   threatening
        and no

(momma)

8

Dizzy Me

If you walk with me, you walk in light.
JOHN 8:12

If you walk in the darkness, you do not know where you are going.
JOHN 12:35 NRSV

To sin is to be blind and dizzy in a pitch-black room. A bit disorienting to say the least. Life with God is a life of clarity, a life of walking in light. To sin? To miss the mark is to embrace confusion, to walk in darkness, to lose all sense of direction.

Jesus pulled no punches. *I am the light,* he said. *If you walk with me, you walk in light* (John 8:12). But if you don't walk with Jesus? *If you walk in the darkness, you do not know where you are going* (John 12:35 NRSV).

To sin is to ignore this light, to choose darkness instead. As the world dims and dims around us, confusion settles over our minds and spirits. Eventually spiritual vertigo sets in. We mistake walls for doors and trees for people. We start a painful collection of emotional and spiritual bruises as we bump and trip our way around life.

Jesus probably smiled at his followers when he confidently proclaimed, *I am the good shepherd* (John 10:11).

Consider the sheep. A dumb animal, really. The one thing a sheep can do well is follow the voice of its master. Stay near him and things are good. Green pastures, flowing streams, the whole bit!

> The shepherd goes out before his sheep, and the sheep follow him for they know his voice. A stranger they will not follow, but they will flee from him, for they do not know the voice of strangers. (John 10:4-5)

Now, consider the runaway sheep. Confused, shortsighted, blind to wolves and cliffs and jagged rocks. The runaway sheep dumbly fumbles his way around.

If he trips and falls on his side, he could lie there and die, never knowing why the field has suddenly gone sideways. He has absolutely no capacity, in and of himself, to regain his equilibrium.

While still upright, he follows his nose. And his nose doesn't know much. Look up the word *clueless* in any dictionary in heaven and you will see there a picture of the lone sheep. The *sheep without a shepherd* was a common metaphor used in the Hebrew Scriptures. (See for yourself in verses such as Numbers 27:17; 1 Kings 22:17; 2 Chronicles 18:16 and Isaiah 13:14.) A metaphor to describe someone hopelessly lost and helpless. *Jesus was sad, for they were like sheep without a shepherd* (Mark 6:34).

At times panic almost sets in: that shaky feeling of having no idea where we are or which way is up. The sharp fear of a lost child finds its way into our grown-up hearts, and we just want everything to make sense—

for the wildly spinning room to just stop, for the sun to rise again.

A sheep needs a shepherd. We always will. And to sin is to ignore that shepherd. To sin is to become woefully lost and confused. Jesus made it clear. *I am the path. I am your light. I am your shepherd and guide.* To miss the mark is to close our eyes and start wandering. Without a path, without sight, without any correct bearings. To sin is to spin in circles till we don't know what's up, what's down or where in the world we are heading!

CAN'T SEE STRAIGHT

Jesus tried to woo the dizzy folks he met walking on the streets around him. *I am the way,* he reasoned (John 14:6 NRSV). *I am the light of this world* (John 8:12).

Jesus read proudly in the synagogue from the book of the prophet Isaiah, *The Spirit of the Lord is upon me . . . to proclaim recovery of sight to the blind.*

His comment on these words? *Today this scripture has been fulfilled in your hearing* (Luke 4:18-21). To obey our shepherd is to have clarity and vision and correct bearings. It is to receive our sight and know spiritual equilibrium.

To sin is to put our vision askew. Like a person who lays his fingers down on a computer keyboard one key too far right and types *kidy s noy pgg* ("just a bit off"). It's not a very big mistake. But everything that he types will be gibberish.

As I sin, my decisions and discernment become more and more suspect. My ideas less clear. It's as if each time I sin my soul spins wildly. Soon I'm disoriented and get a soul headache.

My days become filled with half-truths and guesses as to where I am and what step I should take next. And it only spirals down from there. I start making silly decisions, mistaking good things for bad and vice versa. I end up more bruised than I was to begin with.

Consider King David, an intelligent, godly, clear-minded man who went dizzy, big-time (2 Samuel 11:1-24).

First, a small mistake: David decides to stay in a town full of old men and a lot of women, when he should have been out at war.

Consider his seemingly innocent stroll upon his roof. He lingers, he lusts, he covets. A small act, of course. Long-distance sinning, if you will. His small sin way up there on that roof couldn't affect anyone, right?

But it could. Because that one sin dizzies his soul and the next of a whole series of unthinkable acts happens: he invites Bathsheba over for dinner!

Oh, David. His soul spins and the world blurs and he has his way with her. And the soul nausea only increases until a good man lies murdered and his wife stolen. All this from a seemingly unimportant sin.

All this because sin inherently disorients us. All this because sin dizzies us and leaves us blind and confused, taking shaky steps in directions we never would have imagined.

When I choose to actively covet the possessions and gifts of others, I'm not being bad nearly so much as I'm spinning in quick circles. I'm left dizzy and not seeing quite right. Theft starts to blur, and I step nearer to stealing than I ever thought I could. What used to look like a friend begins to blur and starts looking like an enemy who owns what I want. Anger and bitterness soon grow out of my heart's confusion. And lies and insults will certainly not be far behind.

When I choose to gossip about the fellow down the hall out of jealousy or anger (rather than seeking to wash his feet out of humility, as Jesus suggests), my grip on reality starts to slip. Soon seemingly innocent gossip turns to bitter anger. My venom builds, and his small, harmless acts seem outrageous and idiotic to my dizzy eyes.

If at any time I were to simply "hit the mark" and love him in humility, I would restore sanity to my soul.

But as I continue to miss the mark, his simple human quirks infuriate me, and my venom grows—until the day it all spills out in an angry, biting comment as we pass each other in the hall. And the smell of rancid vinegar fills the air around us. And he sulks off with a surprised, hurt look in his eyes and his tail between his legs! (And I thought I was a nice guy. Wow. I wonder what happened.)

Well, sin happened. To sin is to lose all sight, all bearings on reality. And we become dizzy, confused, scraped-up people. Our souls are battered. We are all bruise and concussion and dizziness. That is what sin is like.

This is the smell of sin, according to Jesus.

SNAKE RIVER CORRECTIONAL FACILITY

Released.

After 26 years of unconscious living in a
cement square of shame and rape and boredom:
a haircut, a used suit, a lead on a small job.
 (And the world in front of him.)

Released.

Released,
but he comes back on weekends.
He lingers outside the cold fence with its sharp razor wire.
He gazes in at his old
cement square of shame and rape and boredom.

Released. (And the world in front of him.)
But he comes back on weekends.

The guards shrug
and slowly shake their heads.

9

Playing in the Grave

> *Jesus cried out with a loud voice,*
> *"Lazarus, come out!"*
>
> JOHN 11:43
>
> *The dead man came out, his hands*
> *and feet bound with bandages, and his*
> *face wrapped with a cloth.*
>
> JOHN 11:44

Sin is inappropriate. Unseemly even.

Not just inappropriate like elbows on the dinner table. Not an inappropriate that would get you stares and cleared throats from more civilized folks. An inappropriate much worse than all that.

Sin is unnatural, like a live man wanting to hang out in tombs and snuggle with coffins. Like a month-old child trying to crawl back into the womb. Like a released prisoner milling about by his dank old prison on weekends. Like a patient who had successful knee surgery refusing to ever try walking again.

Unseemly. Unnatural. Inappropriate.

Jesus was always very clear that entering his kingdom was a massive, total spiritual transformation.

Consider his words to a bewildered Pharisee named Nicodemus:

Very truly, I tell you, no one can enter the kingdom of
God without being born of water and Spirit. What is
born of the flesh is flesh, and what is born of the Spirit
is spirit. (John 3:5-6 NRSV)

Once Jesus saves us with his boundless grace made
possible by the cross, we step over a threshold and enter
a whole new existence. We are new creations. We are re-
made. Our identity, allegiance, purpose, nature and destiny are forever altered. We are born all over again.

Jesus invites all of us to *live* in that reality. Don't just
say you're a new creation. Live like it. We *are* new creations. We are people who are no longer in debt. We
were dead but are alive again. We have been released
from bondage, and we should act like it. We should let
the nearly unfathomable work of the cross settle into
our hands and feet, into our days and weeks.

We are like Lazarus.

Jesus had two commands for Lazarus. His first was
Lazarus, come out! That is the beautiful call of salvation. Come forth from the grave! Be alive! Forever cross
a life-changing threshold (John 11:43)!

And Lazarus did come out. Alive, even. But he
looked weird.

*The dead man came out, his hands and feet bound
with bandages and his face wrapped with a cloth* (John
11:44). Alive? Oh, yes, he was definitely alive. Walking,
talking—the whole bit. Respiration? Check. Circula-
tion? Check. All systems were go. But something was
not quite right.

The problem? Lazarus was still dressed like a dead
man. Oh, Lazarus, wearing grave clothes even though
you're alive now and walking about the room? It's not

just tacky, it's seriously inappropriate. It's . . . *unnatural!* So Jesus had a second, apt command:

> Get out of those grave clothes! Take off the tight, binding death bandages—they are not needed anymore! (John 11:44)

This second call is the call of sanctification. The call to live fully in the miraculous reality Jesus has made possible for us. Salvation and sanctification: the dual call we see illustrated in Jesus' interaction with the woman caught in adultery. "Then neither do I condemn you [salvation]. Go now and leave your life of sin [sanctification]" (John 8:11).

Once this woman sat underneath the saving, calm grace of Jesus, her old life just no longer fit. She was clean and new.

MORE COMFORTABLE?

This sanctification, this unwrapping of the grave clothes, this walking more and more fully in God's will for us, is a beautiful thing. The alternative, continuing to live as if you were the old creation? It is quite ludicrous.

Just imagine. What if Lazarus had hesitated to part with his grave clothes? *Oh, Jesus. Can't I just leave them on for a while? I've kind of gotten used to them. They fit so well!* (Jesus just stares at him blankly.) *No? Well, at least the bandage around my face—can't I just keep that?*

Or what if Lazarus had come back to Jesus a week later. *Hey, Jesus, I'm just going to go back and lie down in the tomb for a while, OK?* (Again, Jesus looks a bit confused.) *Oh, not forever. I like being alive and all. Thanks again, Jesus, for . . . you know, raising me from the dead and all! I just want to hang out there for a little while, take*

a nap in the dark . . . maybe snuggle with those bandages
you made them take away from me . . .

What should his sisters, Martha and Mary, say to the
many visitors who've come miles to meet "the one who
was dead—but is alive again"? Would they have to
shrug their shoulders and clear their throats awkwardly? Would their eyes roll in disdain as they ex-
plained to the visitors, "Well, he's not actually here in
the house, he's sleeping in that tomb he was dead in."
(More shrugs.) "It's right over there."

That would be ludicrous. Totally inappropriate. Like
longing for Snake River Correctional Facility after being
released. It's great to come alive. Amen for salvation.
But it's also great to live as alive men and women!

Listen to Paul as he urges the Colossian Christians
not to sin. He explains that they should stop sinning
so much because *you have stripped off the old self*
with its practices and have clothed yourselves with
the new self, which is being renewed in knowledge ac-
cording to the image of its creator (Colossians 3:9-10
NRSV). He reasons with them to pursue holiness, describing it as "putting on" the things of God (Colossians 3:12). A changed heart and eternal destiny
require a change in clothes.

James expresses the need for sanctification in this way:

> But be doers of the word, and not merely hearers who
> deceive themselves. For if any are hearers of the word
> and not doers, they are like those who look at them-
> selves in a mirror; for they look at themselves and, on
> going away, immediately forget what they were like.
> (James 1:22-24 NRSV)

Jesus has changed who we are. And we are called to live in light of who we really are. We shouldn't forget this amazing transformation that has come over us. We shouldn't forget what our image in the mirror says about who we are. We shouldn't go on living as dead people.

Again, Paul urged the Ephesians to *put away your former way of life, your old self, corrupt and deluded . . . and to be renewed* (Ephesians 4:22 NRSV). Put it off, he says, it doesn't fit anymore!

When I sin, I'm not just being silly and naughty. I'm not just goofing around. I'm not sneaking into a great amusement park. I'm playing in the grave. I'm forgetting what my new face looks like. I'm refusing to put off my grave clothes like I should. I just get up in the morning and put on my old clothes and act like the dead all around me who've not been reborn in Jesus.

In the light of all that Jesus has done for me and in me, that's a gross choice. It's like eating rocks instead of watermelon. His act on the cross has changed me, and naturally it should be changing how I am and how I live. When I sin, I disregard the transformation I've been through.

SLOW LEARNER

Consider Jesus' story of the unmerciful servant (Matthew 18:23-35). Here we hear of a servant who owes an impossible amount of money. The king wants to reconcile accounts, so he calls in the debt. The servant falls on his face, sobbing, pleading for forgiveness of the debt. It's an impossible amount for him to repay, after all.

So the king forgives the debt. He has compassion and wipes the slate clean! Just like that. It's an amazing grace.

A great story except for one thing. The man does the most ridiculous thing. Instead of basking in the forgiveness given him, he runs into a fellow servant who owes him a little money—and he sends him to debtor's prison! Jesus' story then ends with a resounding *What!?*

> When his fellow slaves saw what had happened, they were greatly distressed, and they went and reported to their lord all that had taken place. Then his lord summoned him and said to him, "You wicked slave! I forgave you all that debt because you pleaded with me. Should you not have had mercy on your fellow slave, as I had mercy on you? (Matthew 18:31-33 NRSV)

When we sin, God doesn't just click his tongue and roll his eyes in frustration. He's as dumbfounded as the king in the parable. As incredulous as the guards at the Snake River Correctional Facility. *I've done this amazing thing for you, I've transformed you! And you're doing what?! You're still living like dead people? Take off those grave clothes and live!*

When I tell small lies, or ignore a beautiful call in Scripture, I am closing my eyes to all that God has done for me. The writer of Hebrews might say I'm trampling the Son of God underfoot, treating as an unholy thing the blood of the covenant, even insulting the Spirit of grace (Hebrews 10:29).

When I ignore my neighbor (instead of loving him or her as Jesus commands), I am rolling around in my old grave clothes, rather than living as a new creation.

When I choose bitterness and hatred in a hard relationship, rather than choosing grace and forgiveness, I am forgetting (or blatantly ignoring) what my soul really looks like, what kind of new life I have been born into.

When we sin, we are forgetting who we are. We are turning our back in unnatural mockery at Jesus' suffering and death. We are like healthy men and women spending our time in a grave that's meant for decaying corpses.

That is the smell of sin, according to Jesus.

BUBBLE CONSTRUCTION COMPANY®
(PRIME TIME AD #34C)

[Pan shot of dejected young couples sitting in a dirt field.]

> Voice Over (an impressive, deeply resonate voice):
> Tired of dreaming about owning a home?
> Ready to become a proud Home Owner?

[Focus in on one couple. They look up, their eyes widen with hope.]

> Maybe you're ready to consider . . .
> one of our incredible . . . Inflatable Houses!

[Music begins. The wife jumps up and squeals as a pink Bubble Construction Company® van drives around the corner, soap bubbles and happy music floating out of the open windows.]

> Cheap! Easy! And . . .
> (if you have a Bubble Construction Company®
> Joy7 Air Compressor) . . . quick to blow up!

[The husband hugs his wife, stands tall and proud . . . she gazes up at him with a suggestive smile.]

> Just imagine . . . you could be living in your very
> own Inflatable House . . .
> today!

[Various scenes of the couple laughing, flirting and enjoying their Inflatable House.]

> Remember, with the Bubble Construction Company®:
> [Jingle music begins.]

> "We make it . . . you inflate it!"

10

A Carpenter's Nightmare

> *Everyone who comes to me and hears my words and does them, I will show you what he is like: he is like a man building a house on rock. No weather can shake that house.*
>
> LUKE 6:47-48

> *But he who hears my words but does not do them is like a man who builds a house on sand. The weather will completely destroy that house.*
>
> LUKE 6:49

Sin is horrendous carpentry. It erodes stability.

Jesus said that life with him—lived according to his good plan—was a sure, solid thing. What is it like to hit the mark? Jesus painted the picture of a wise man building a stable house.

This man begins with the knowledge that progress can be a deceptive thing. Sure, he wants to build a tall house, he wants to see the framing go up and the walls become towering! He dreams of having a roof over his head for shade and shelter. He can hardly wait to put the finishing touches on the paint and stand back and say, "I just built a house!"

But this wise man, who obeys the words of Jesus, knows

that progress is not always a thrilling, exciting thing.

So he starts to dig. A lot. (With only his hands and a shovel, back in Jesus' day: no big yellow tractors to be found.) His goal? Dig through the rough ground until the hard soil gives way to impossibly hard rock. How deep? Depends on where the rock lies.

Could be weeks. His neighbors are throwing up homes with ease and joy! He is digging a hole.

Actually, he can barely see his neighbors' homes anymore as he stands deep within the earth, bending over to pull out dirt clods, watching his shovel strike the deep, dark soil again and again, wiping the sweat off his face.

But in the end, his home is built. And he has shade, and shelter, and a place to rest. Just like his neighbors.

Oh, weather happens from time to time. Sure it does. He can hear the rain and wind beating furiously against his walls and roof as he sits calmly in his kitchen, eating breakfast and reading the paper.

Sure, weather happens. He just stays inside on those days. He has a home. And peace of mind. His life is stable.

To obey Jesus is to build something solid, a life that's sturdy and right and good. The stuff of this world cannot tear it down.

The wise man can breathe a deep sigh of relief with the psalmist who wrote, *He drew me up from the desolate pit, out of the miry bog, and set my feet upon a rock, making my steps secure* (Psalm 40:2 NRSV).

To live in righteousness is to live on a rock. It is ultimate security.

So, what's it like to sin, to miss the mark? Jesus says it's a lot easier. And much more foolish. (A little like buying an inflatable house!)

Jesus asks us to picture a man who finds a plot with flat ground and a great view, so he throws up a house.

It's a real house. Walls, doors, windows. Even has a back deck! And the best thing is, it's a house that's easy to build. Not long after finding the plot of ground, the house is up and you're kicking back on the deck enjoying the view!

The only problem? This house is built on a beach. On nice smooth sand. It has no foundation. And, sure, weather happens. And, of course, the house is utterly destroyed. It has a "great fall," Jesus says. And there is no house left.

QUICK 'N' DIRTY

That's what it's like according to Jesus. The temptation to sin is, indeed, a temptation to ease and light work and quick pleasure. To sin is to have a life that looks like many other lives. To sin is to "progress" quickly.

But ultimately, there is nothing. It is all swept away with the inevitable weather that life brings. No house at all. Just shattered windows, flattened walls and a mangled, crushed pile of wood that used to be a deck.

It'd be so much easier to believe that not obeying Jesus was like splattering paint on a wall. A spot. A silly stain that speaks of disobedience, that brings on shame. A mere cosmetic problem. It's so much harder to believe that missing the mark is setting myself up for a great fall—that sin is not a surface thing but a deep, structural core problem.

When I spend all of my energy and resources on myself and ignore Jesus' call to care for the poor and lift up those in need, am I simply attracting the disappointed look of the teacher? Or am I building a shallow, fragile life? Am I being a terrible carpenter whose life has a "great fall" in its future?

Consider the life of Paul.

Now this is a man who knew about weather. All kinds of storms pounded against the house of his life. The authorities, whole towns, even nature itself tried everything to knock him down: stonings, beatings, snake bites, shipwrecks, arrests—the man faced some severe weather!

But Paul's house stayed up. Listen in on his letter to a timid young believer:

> Now you have observed my teaching, my conduct, my aim in life, my faith, my patience, my love, my steadfastness, my persecutions and suffering the things that happened to me in Antioch, Iconium, and Lystra. What persecutions I endured! Yet the Lord rescued me from all of them. (2 Timothy 3:10-11 NRSV)

Paul's life was a picture of a house with a solid foundation. It could face all kinds of storms. He knew that, and he had no problem inviting other people to live that same kind of life, because he knew it was the only secure, sturdy, sure life around.

Consider Herod Antipas. This man staked his foundation on appearances and on the approval of those around him. He had John the Baptist arrested—to appease his wife, Herodias. He couldn't go ahead and kill John, because he was afraid of John. At his birthday party he promised his stepdaughter anything she wanted—because he wanted to impress his aroused guests. And when she demanded John's head on a platter (thanks for the idea, Herodias) Herod could only relent, because he didn't want to look foolish in front of his guests (Mark 6:14-29).

Herod's life was built on a weak foundation: the flattery of others. His life was a series of shaky, fragile moves dictated by others' thoughts and whims. He had a life, all right. Lots of folks probably envied his position and money—the bright paint and fancy shingles of his house. But his life didn't go anywhere or produce anything solid. It was fragile and shaky, and in the end it fell down. Eventually deposed from his throne, he spent the remainder of his life in exile. After all is said and done, the thoughts and whims of others do not make a very lasting foundation in the storms of life.

When I idolize anything above God (be it sports, philosophy or food) I'm not just being "silly and disobedient." *Do not have idols before me* (Exodus 20:3) is not a mere trifle or random technicality. It is a mark, a target. Hitting it will lead me to stability. Missing it will bring me down. To idolize money or people or anything at all is to invite seepage into my life. It is not a choice to be seen as "naughty" but a choice that invites spiritual and emotional wobbliness. It's a disaster waiting to happen.

To live for money is not just a bit shameful because our green greed is embarrassing for God. No. To live for money is to build a fragile, hazardous life. A life of greed doesn't just offend Jesus' humble nature—it shocks and bewilders his instincts as a carpenter.

So he asks us to picture the destruction that bad carpentry leads to. He wants us to smell the salt water surging over shredded linoleum and mangled gutters. The smell of destruction. The smell of instability. Of false hopes and false security and false ease. Salt water washing over utterly splintered wood.

This is the smell of sin, according to Jesus.

SMILING ADDICT

He smiles.
He struts.
He flirts with the ladies.

He is all laughter and winks and cocky insults
        as he strolls,
                Kingly,
        down the avenue.

        In the alley behind Walgreens
        G-Note will take food stamps
                (50 cents on the dollar)
        for your favorite diversion.

        He is all smiles in the alley behind Walgreens.
        He laughs   Royally.
        His head is held high.
        He is a   King.

The next morning there is no smile
        as he stumbles
back to an apartment nearly emptied into hock
and a wife   who doesn't look up,
and a daughter (in her bedroom)
                who cringes
when she hears her father's
voice.

11

Life with Chains

> *If you continue in my word, . . . the truth will make you free.*
>
> JOHN 8:31-32 NRSV

> *Very truly, I tell you, everyone who commits sin is a slave to sin.*
>
> JOHN 8:34 NRSV

To sin is to be a slave.

Not a servant, a slave.

Sin parades itself as ultimate freedom, ultimate self-expression. Our moment of being an individual! It's like the kid who musters the courage to throw the paper airplane toward the blackboard, directly at the teacher's turned back. In a moment of glorious freedom, he has his way! Oh, he'll probably get caught. He'll have to serve detention and return to boring subservience. But for now he screams those two syllables along with Mel Gibson in *Braveheart:* "FREE-DOM!!!"

A lie. A complete deception.

Jesus came with a message of freedom: *If you follow me, you'll be free! And anyone whom I make free is free indeed* (John 8:36).

We start enslaved. And Jesus comes as Savior, as

Superman to break our chains and set us free! *I have come to proclaim release to the captives, to set at liberty those who are oppressed* (Luke 4:18).

To follow Jesus, to live in his will is to be set free.

Sin? To sin is to return to captivity. As Paul put it, *For freedom Christ has set us free. Stand firm, therefore, and do not submit again to a yoke of slavery* (Galatians 5:1 NRSV).

But *we* aren't slaves, we protest. We are the ones in control! When I sin, it's me doing the choosing. I'm no slave!

The Pharisees' pride and delusion match our own. To Jesus' offer of freedom, they protested loudly, *But we are sons of Abraham! We have never been slaves to anyone. To anyone!*

Jesus' reply? It was short and stark. *Truly, truly, I say to you, anyone who commits sin is a slave to sin* (John 8:33-34). Anyone.

No vague words to hide behind. No attractive pictures of children's desks or tall Ferris wheels. Jesus tells us that if we want to know something about the true smell of sin, we should conjure up images of slavery.

To sin is to be in bondage, he says. To have your ankles shackled with rusty iron circles that are held fast with the strongest of chains. To sin is to have your sandals and khakis and Gap T-shirt stripped away, to have your hands bound with tight ovals of iron. To sin is to be led away by a cruel, sweaty man in black leather who frowns and spits. He is a large man. His whip flies at will, and the ripped flesh never has time to heal. The leather cords always cut, and the blood always flows.

The blood drenches the rusty iron and the smell weakens your knees.

To sin is to be led to a dungeon where perpetual night reigns and the quick motions and sickly sounds in the muck at your feet can't be identified. You don't even want to know what's there, what keeps slipping over your bare, bloody feet.

When you're a slave, you rarely eat.

It seems like you're always working in the mines. The endless pain of the deep, dark mines makes your room in the dungeon seem like a pleasant getaway.

And as your days and nights blur into a continuous reality of pain and hunger and blood, you almost forget that word chiseled cruelly into your iron shackles. *Freedom*.

SWEAT AND BURNED FLESH

This is the smell of sin. Iron and blood and old leather. The smell of sweat and burned flesh. The downcast eyes, the beaten and bruised face. This is what sin is like. Not some frowning, disappointed teacher in a classroom.

Oh, how a slave would long for a classroom! With its gentle, whispering children and the lights overhead and the dry, clean floor beneath! But no. The slave is not in control. He cannot choose where to be, only what to dream of, what delusions to entertain.

He is controlled. Like our smiling drug addict who feigns power and choice, so a man becomes an addict to sin. And loses control.

If you sin, you become a slave to sin. No wonder Jesus said we'd be better off gnawing off a hand than having that hand lead us into sin. No wonder.

There *is* no polite classroom. There is a dungeon, and there is a slave master.

When I am tempted by some attractive little sin, I am never considering an innocent splurge. I am holding shackles to my own ankles, considering whether or not to clasp the iron shut.

When a man chooses to actively lust, to "indulge" in pornography, he is not choosing only to gratify his desires. He is choosing to have his hands bound so tightly that he can't move about freely anymore.

When a woman makes the choice to subtly seduce her neighbor's husband, she is not choosing to feel acceptance and belonging and joy. She is becoming a slave. She is losing control of her life.

Consider my friend in Texas who pulled me aside one day and confided (for the first time to another Christian) that he had been going to strip bars for years and couldn't stop. He is a strong man, a follower of Jesus. But he is bound. He is a slave.

Consider his seemingly innocent beginnings: the eyes that lingered in public places, the soft porn, the driving around the block five times before pulling in to a strip bar for the first time. My friend is not being *naughty*. No. That's not the smell in his life at all. The shaky tone in his voice and the darting eyes as he talks would tell you that much. He is a slave.

Consider the rich young ruler.

He longed to know what to do to have eternal life. So he found an audience with Jesus himself. He talked, face to face, with our dear Jesus. Imagine!

Well, they got to talking about this man's life, and about his active pursuit of holiness. And there must have been something about this man that really struck Jesus. Is it possible that Jesus would have another disciple to add to his inner circle? Just maybe. Listen to the invitation Jesus gave him.

> Jesus, looking at him, loved him and said, "You lack one thing; go, sell what you own, and give the money to the poor, and you will have treasure in heaven; then come, follow me." (Mark 10:21 NRSV)

Wow. What a fantastic invitation. But it would seem that this man had an idolatrous leaning towards money. (Someday, check out for yourself which of the ten commandments Jesus leaves out of his list!) So the story grinds to an end: *When he heard this he was shocked and went away grieving, for he had many possessions* (Mark 10:22 NRSV).

It's a picture of slavery, of a man who is no longer in control of his life, isn't it? After all, why did he walk away? Not because he felt Jesus had misread his attitude toward money. Not because he had pressing engagements. And certainly not because he wasn't really interested in following Jesus. He hated to walk away. (How would they know he was "sorrowful" as he left, if not for tears and a look of longing?)

The biblical account says he couldn't do what he wanted for one reason: *for he had great possessions.* His idolatry turned him into a slave. He was no longer in control.

When I sin, I am not just bravely asserting my own freedom. I am handing over my freedom to a big, sweaty man whose eyes are bent on cruelty. I am not assuring myself forbidden pleasure nearly as much as I am assuring myself slavery and addiction and chains.

This is the smell of sin, according to Jesus.

OUT, OUT, PESKY SPOT!

If your nose is bleeding,
Don't just take your shirt to the cleaners.

12

The Stench Within

> *The good person out of the good
> treasure of the heart produces good,
> and the evil person out of evil treasure
> produces evil.*
>
> LUKE 6:45 NRSV

> *For from within, out of the heart of
> man, comes evil.*
>
> MARK 7:21

The smell is bad. It's really bad.

In the full view of Scripture the lies shrivel up and want to slink back to the caves from whence they came. We might be tempted to laugh at them, had they not deceived us so. But Jesus murders these lies with an ugly gang of graphic facts. Jesus says sin is a deep insult. It chokes us and dizzies us and cruelly enslaves us. Sin makes a fragile, precarious thing out of our lives.

Sin echoes in our lives. A deadly, toxic echo. And throughout the Gospels Jesus, without apology, starkly describes for us this stench of sin.

But there is one more point that Jesus was very clear about. That smell, that stench that smacks of death and slavery and insult, is coming from INSIDE US.

Sin is a sickness. And this sickness lives in our hearts.

Not only is the smell of sin much worse than we ever really believed, the truly bad news is that this stench is coming from inside our deepest parts. We are not *stained* with sin near as much as we are *infected* by it. Oh, it's worse than we had ever thought.

In Jesus' day, the Pharisees were diligent and dutiful to keep their outsides clean. They complained to Jesus one day because (gasp!) his disciples were eating a meal without first having washed their hands! Wouldn't that make them "unclean" and "impure"? Wasn't that missing the mark?

Jesus looked at his disciples' dirty hands, looked back at these bitter, violent Pharisees and could only sigh and plead with them, *Listen to me, all of you, and understand: there is nothing outside a person that by going in can defile, but the things that come out are what defile* (Mark 7:14-15 NRSV).

Of course, no one understood what Jesus was talking about. Sin is all external, right? To eat with unclean hands, to physically commit adultery, to strike a man's cheek, to utter a lie—it's these external things that are the problem, right?

Thankfully, later that same day Jesus' followers privately asked him about this mysterious "parable" he had taught. They, too, were utterly confused about the location of the smell.

Jesus was forced to get blunt for his disciples:

Things that enter you from outside cannot defile you—because they don't enter your heart! They just enter your stomach, and then you expel them. No real problem.

> The real problem is what comes out of you. For from
> within, out of the heart of men, come evil thoughts, for-
> nication, theft, murder, adultery, coveting, wickedness,
> deceit, licentiousness, envy, slander, pride, foolishness.
> All these evil things come from within, and they defile
> a man. (Mark 7:18-23)

Here, where we finally get some sort of list of sins,
Jesus confronts us with the stark reality that sin resides
within our hearts. When we sin it's not just a problem of
being naughty, it's a case of being sick, being utterly infected by a disease.

Sin is always a heart problem.

Imagine a man with a broken nose furiously scrubbing the blood from his shirt while ignoring his nose,
and you've got a decent picture of what we're often like.

We scrub and scrub that shirt trying to get it clean
again! But the blood keeps dripping down from our nose.
And the shirt ever remains bloody. Because the problem
is not with our shirt, really. The problem is with our nose.
Or with our *hearts*, to get more to the point.

Jesus tried to make this clear to his agriculturally
minded followers.

> For no good tree bears bad fruit, nor again does a bad
> tree bear good fruit; for each tree is known by its own
> fruit. (Luke 6:43-44)

Wouldn't it be silly to see an orchard worker going,
daily, to a cherry tree to see if there were any *apples*
yet?! *Silly tree*, he thinks. *It keeps putting out cherries.
What a ridiculous apple tree!*

No. What a ridiculous orchard worker. The fruit on
the outside is merely a reflection of what is on the in-

side. And as it is with fruit trees, so it is with men and women, according to Jesus. If you see sin on the outside, you know exactly what's on the inside.

Sin is no cleanly laminated list of rules. It is no alluring but off-limits amusement park. And it is far, far from being a silly myth.

The more I read Jesus' teachings on sin, the more gaping I realize my theology has been. Not only have I been deceived about the smell of sin, but also about where that smell is coming from.

As it turns out, when I sin I am not a naughty school boy. I am a diseased man. And the symptoms are frightening.

I am a rebellious son, an unfaithful spouse. I choke my own neck and dizzy my own head. My whole life becomes tenuous and fragile, and the sturdiest thing to come of my sin is the stout iron that shackles my arms and legs and soul.

I'm not naughty. I'm a fool. I am unfaithful and weak and oppressed.

This, Jesus says, *this* is the smell of sin. And wherever you go—there the stench is.

Thus teaches our dear, sweet Jesus.

BOOK FOUR

The Fresh Air of Grace

In which we celebrate

the surprising beauty that

accompanies the true

smell of sin.

QUICK TRIGGER FINGER

There is a lie
living in an old dark green shoe box
in the back of my bedroom closet.

In this old shoe box
    live piles
        of unsorted, slightly bent photos
of my childhood.

And in every picture
    the clear ones and the blurry ones
    the Polaroids and the 35mm's
    the cold winter shots and sunny summer ones
I am smiling.

In every one.

13
Cry

> *Blessed are those who mourn, for they
> will be comforted.*
>
> MATTHEW 5:4 NRSV

What's a sinner to do?

If sin were just a naughty prank, we could straighten up and fly right. We could just knock off all of the horseplay.

But sin is not like that. Jesus says it is an addictive, toxic, infesting thing. And we need help.

The truth is we need Jesus. Like the lepers and paralytics and wounded of his own day, we need the help of this carpenter who people claim can heal a person. We desperately need him to come through for us.

The truth is, knowing the reality of sin—the real smell of it—should not depress and deflate us; it should make us mourn our sins and cry out for help. And crying out, in the kingdom of God, is a beautiful thing.

Not so in the kingdom of the world. In the world crying out is a shameful, weak thing. Socially, we're taught from a young age to just get it all together. Snot's not cool. And who ever reaches for a camera when someone's crying, anyway? We unconsciously edit our tears from our photo albums.

And in today's world where no one is ever morally

guilty for anything, why would anyone ever need to bother "mourning" their actions?

We swim in a societal ethic that tells us feeling bad is wrong. All pricked consciences must be checked at the door. Feeling "convicted" or "guilty" is to be avoided at all costs these days. Even in the church we are quick to smooth over confessions and quickly encourage anyone who—heaven forbid!—feels he or she has sinned. The result is that true, clear conviction can be a rare occurrence for many of us.

It's all OK. This is the soothing mantra that our modern culture uses to pet us every chance it gets. *It's all OK. Don't worry. Don't fret. It's all just . . . OK.*

Perhaps we no longer know what it means to repent because we no longer know what it means to have sinned.

Even our language betrays us. We don't sin; we "have issues" or we "struggle with sin." But that's just not true, is it? We don't *have issues* like some fast-food manager trying to work out employee spats. What we have is a sinful heart. And we certainly don't *struggle with sin*, as we are so quick to say. We don't struggle at all, usually. Sometimes we sin at will, with vigor.

The fact is, you and I do sin. We need to just sit still and truly feel the import of that. To feel it, raw and painful, without being immediately calmed or soothed or talked out of it. We need to re-learn how to blush.

The work of the Spirit—one of the main reasons Jesus sent his Counselor—is to convict us of our sins, so that we might feel a holy conviction (John 16:8). It's a right thing to feel. *Compunction*, the Puritans called it. A weird word, but it's Jesus' intention that we would feel it. That we would cry. That we would mourn. That we would feel, deeply and in painful detail, the poverty of our spirits. And find, then, what it is to have our Lord lift us out of our mourning.

THE UP SIDE

The true smell of sin frees us from the smooth, suffocating lies of this age. Smelling sin doesn't beat us down, it opens doors for us!

Perhaps this is why Jesus felt it was so important for us to have clarity on the smell of sin. Talk of repentance and grace and forgiveness rings hollow if sin is just an arbitrary list of fun things we're not supposed to do.

We do not demean grace when we feel guilty for our sins, when we feel true compunction. This crying, this "bad" feeling is the stuff of the gospel itself. It's these other familiar, false smells that cheapen grace and rip away from us the chance to bravely mourn and cleanly repent of our sins.

Jesus said it is the poor in spirit who are lucky, because they are the ones who really see. They see the true reality of their hearts and can go to Jesus for help.

They are blessed, he said (Matthew 5:3).

If we keep believing what the world says about the smell of sin, then we will never know what it is to be poor in spirit. Sure, we'll still feel naughty or guilty from time to time, and we'll utter a prayer or two so that those feelings will go away. But we won't know true poverty of spirit.

Consider Jesus' teaching.

Two men went up to the temple to pray, one a Pharisee and the other a tax collector. The Pharisee, standing by himself, was praying thus, "God, I thank you that I am not like other people: thieves, rogues, adulterers, or even like this tax collector. I fast twice a week; I give a tenth of all my income." But the tax collector, standing far off, would not even look up to heaven, but was beating his breast and saying, "God, be merciful to me, a sinner!" I tell you, this man went down to his house justified rather than the other. (Luke 18:10-14 NRSV)

It was the mournful man, the one who really felt the reality of his sins, who—in the very words of Jesus—*went down to his house justified.*

In this world of résumés, GPAs and feel-good psychology, we need to relearn this holy posture of being on our knees before God.

In Jesus' own day it was those who knew their poor state who sought Jesus out, who ran around lakes to be near him and fall at his feet. It was the desperate who longed for just a touch from Jesus and were willing to risk social outrage to get that touch.

In fact, there's a long list of folks who've found themselves on their knees, like beggars, at the feet of Jesus. This was a common posture in Jesus' day. Fishermen, lepers, prostitutes, Pharisees, soldiers . . . all of them, regardless of station in life or social class, found themselves drawn, humbly, to the feet of Jesus.

Those who felt they were just fine? They just ignored him. (Until he got intrusive and powerful, of course.) The seemingly righteous had no perceived need for Jesus, so he could do nothing for them.

It's almost as if Jesus is reserved for those in desperate need. This frustrated lots of folks in Jesus' day. Why wasn't this popular new teacher talking with them, the truly worthy? So they asked, *Why does he eat with tax collectors and sinners?*

And Jesus answered, *Those who are well have no need of a physician, but those who are sick; I have come not to call the righteous but sinners* (Mark 2:17 NRSV).

A HOLY POSTURE

It is a holy posture to be on your knees, pleading with Jesus. To be so sick, so desperate that our utter failure is assured if Jesus doesn't come through for us. This posture should be a regular part of our life of following Jesus. It was commonplace in Jesus' own day; shouldn't it be today too?

I am learning this posture. The more I read Jesus' words on sin (and believe them) the more deeply sober I am becoming. It's an uncomfortable feeling. I am less impressed with myself than I ever have been. It hasn't been an easy conversion for me. Jesus' graphic words make me and my sin look tragic and destructive. His words don't stroke my fragile ego. They cut deep.

I could fight off these feelings, of course. Try to explain away Jesus' graphic words in a way that leaves me untouched and still just harmlessly "naughty" in my sin.

Or I can begin to face reality and be freed from the strong, relativistic opiate of our age. I can smell my sin for what it really is—and find myself running to Jesus. I can join this long, illustrious list of beggars who've fallen at our Beloved's feet in need.

I can learn what it means to cry out in my need. To openly and unabashedly proclaim the strong, freeing truth: *Jesus, I need you.* Yes, I NEED.

I need a counselor who's good at helping people overcome addictions.

I need a rescuer who is good at breaking chains of iron.

I need a physician who works on messed-up hearts—for free.

I need a bright light and a clear path and a strong, sure voice to follow.

I need something more solid than shifting sand undergirding my life.

I need to eat. To be given life-giving food and drink.

The sober, overwhelming reality of my sin drives me to Jesus. A Jesus who did not come for those who feel righteous or merely naughty. A carpenter who, as it turned out, really *was* able to heal a person!

And you know what I'm finding? He still can. He is alive today just as he was then. And he is still a physician. He is still our good, loving shepherd, and he is still light and a path.

He is still a solid rock for us to stand on, he is still our counselor, he is still a lover who forgives his unfaithful bride and a forgiving father who longs to welcome us back and wipe the slate clean.

He is still the life-giving vine in which to abide. And he is still bread and water and exactly, *exactly* what we need.

And we still get to call out to him—just like the people in his own day.

Jesus was not graphic about the reality of sin because he was interested in depressing us. No. Jesus longed for us to know the truth—and longed for us to cry out to him in our need.

> Come to me if you are weary and heavy burdened, and I
> will give you rest. (Matthew 11:28)

If we believe we're just being naughty in the classroom of life, how can we ever hear this beautiful invitation from Jesus? If we believe in lukewarm sin, won't our repentance be lukewarm as well?

No wonder Jesus said it was the poor in spirit, the beggars in spiritual matters, who were blessed and lucky.

No wonder he congratulated those who mourned.

FIELD TRIP

The first time I stood at the edge of the Grand Canyon

I forgot all about my out-of-style haircut,
  became suddenly unconscious of my shameful acne,
   stopped tugging at my cheap, drooping socks,

And smiled.

  For the first time since arriving at
   Bonham Junior High School
  I was utterly deaf to the barbed giggling of
   the popular girls.

I stood and gaped.

14
Worship

> *She stood behind him at his feet,*
> *weeping, and began to bathe his feet*
> *with her tears and to dry them with her*
> *hair. Then she continued kissing his feet*
> *and anointing them with the ointment.*
>
> LUKE 7:38 NRSV

Worship is a beautiful, strange thing.

I wonder if we really know much of how to worship these days. I guess if we have only a tepid, vague understanding of the reality of our sin, then we shouldn't be surprised if our worship is also tepid and vague.

How inspired should we feel if we think Jesus just died to "cover up our tardy slips in the classroom of life"? Not so impressive, is it? If we, along with the world around us, underestimate the smell of sin, then we are also underestimating exactly what Jesus has accomplished for us.

A hero who saves us from the stench and death of slavery—now that's a man I want to find, a man at whose feet I could collapse breathlessly. But someone who saves me from the results of my being naughty? Hmmm. Well, if he's around, I guess I'll thank him, but . . . I don't want to go out of my way or anything.

No wonder worship is awkward for many of us. No wonder our minds quickly focus on the people around us and the musicians and the choice of songs. There's just nothing else too impressive to keep our attention.

As we submit to Jesus' clear teachings about the smell of sin, however, we are finally free to really worship! Thank God.

We realize that the grace of Jesus isn't some petty legal maneuver to help us "settle out of court" with God, so that our small acts of sin aren't held against us. No. It's a thousand times bigger than that. And then some.

Our sins are immense and we are guilty. We are tried and convicted, and it's a death sentence. And our time has come and the guards are stiffly escorting us down the long hallway to the electric chair that rightfully awaits us. Dead men and women walking. And when we round the last corner, the guards simply have to let us go . . . because the chair is already in use. Jesus is in it. And he's being electrocuted.

Now *that's* something to worship about.

A VERY STRANGE AFFAIR

One night Jesus was having dinner at a Pharisee's home, when a prostitute sneaked into the house and starting doing some very strange things.

> A woman in the city, who was a sinner, having learned that he was eating in the Pharisee's house, brought an alabaster jar of ointment. She stood behind him at his feet, weeping, and began to bathe his feet with her tears and to dry them with her hair. Then she continued kissing his feet and anointing them with the ointment. (Luke 7:37-38 NRSV)

Oh, to have been a fly on that wall! I wonder what that evening was really like.

The woman first stood behind Jesus (who was reclining on the ground) and wept. I wonder if the dinner guests saw her first or *heard* her first.

I wonder, how far over did she have to lean to get her face down to Jesus' feet? How *long* did she kneel there weeping? It must have taken a lot of tears to wash both of his dirty feet. Did a salty mud form on Jesus' feet?

And what were the dinner guests doing during this weeping? Were their eyes awkwardly avoiding that side of the room, or were they shamelessly riveted on what was happening?

So many questions.

Did her hair get muddy as she dried his feet? Did she care? What were the kisses like? Where on his feet did she kiss, anyway? The toes? The top? The ankle? Did the smell of ointment immediately fill the room or did the new scent slowly grow?

Wow. What a party!

How awkward this must have been for the woman—to barge uninvited into a roomful of men, interrupt a meal and perform all of these intimate, slow acts of love while the dinner guests probably gawked and coughed nervously.

But no. The awkwardness, the shuffling feet and loudly cleared throats must have been lost on her. She was so enraptured with the carpenter who spoke such love and forgiveness—to even a street woman like her— that she was lost in her emotions. She must have been oblivious to all else in the room.

What a beautiful picture of worship. What a *clear* picture of worship.

The host of the dinner began to complain about her actions, of course. So Jesus, who had silently and calmly received all of her love, felt it important to explain to those in the room what had just gone on.

He felt a short story could best sum it up. *A certain creditor had two debtors; one owed five hundred denarii, the other fifty. When they could not pay, he forgave them both. Now which of them will love him more?*

The host, Simon, answered, *The one, I suppose, to whom he forgave more.*

Exactly.

Exactly. Jesus knew that those who were forgiven much loved much. And looking into the eyes of Simon the indignant Pharisee, Jesus calmly spoke this chilling truth: *The one to whom little is forgiven, loves little* (Luke 7:41-42, 47 NRSV).

He who is forgiven little loves little. So the person who is forgiven simply for being naughty and breaking a rule—is that person able to love only a little too?

The true smell of sin frees us from our petty, lukewarm love for Jesus. It allows us to truly feel the reality of our sins—and truly feel the joy of Jesus' forgiveness!

Consider Levi (Mark 2:14-15). A man hated by almost everyone in his town. A successful tax collector whose success depended on having tough skin, being able to withstand an old woman's pleas for mercy, the tear-filled excuses of a young couple who "just can't" pay their taxes. A hard, successful man.

But when Jesus comes to him and invites him to a life of discipleship (*him*, the hated tax collector), Levi's tough skin and forced postures simply melt away. What is the only thing he can do in response to such forgiveness, such love and acceptance? Just like the prostitute at the Pharisee's house—*something beautiful.*

So, Levi throws an immense party at his house, inviting all his friends (other sinners, of course—the only folks who would dare associate with such a man), and he breathlessly introduces everyone to his new friend Jesus.

TALK ABOUT A 180!

Or consider Zacchaeus (Luke 19:1-10). Another tax collector. Another successful one. But a short man, this one. Surely, a hardened exterior, a chip on the shoulder.

But one encounter with the open arms of Jesus and what can he do? Again, *something beautiful.* So, he has this huge dinner and declares that he will pay back—fourfold—anything he has ever cheated anyone out of. Wow!

Are we noticing a theme here? When Jesus embraced the needy, their sin apparent and large, they could only respond in beauty, in worship of him. And those self-righteous types watching, who thought they were sinless, could only stand around and complain that Jesus was hanging out with the wrong types again!

Jesus' teachings on the seriousness, the foul smell of sin do not weigh us down. They free us to worship!

For me, worship has almost always been awkward. I find my eyes wandering to those around me, wondering about how they're standing or singing or raising their hands. Wondering what they think about how *I'm* standing or singing or raising my hands.

My mind often continues to race along the events of my day, the stuff of life I'm preoccupied with. And for me, the music has always made it difficult. There are guitarists to watch, singers to stare at, certain tunes to dislike, other songs to grow tired of. To be really honest, I'm not sure how much real worship I've done while standing and singing and looking around.

Things are changing, though. (Praise God!)

The more sober I become about my own poverty of spirit, the more impressed I am by Jesus. I'm less impressed with myself, and feeling more and more like a young child. But in the midst of that, the more I follow Jesus and the more I read Scripture, the more *taken* I am with him. The more enthralled I am with his words. The more impressed I am with how he treats people, how he responds to folks in the Gospels, and how he deals with this young child that I am becoming.

There's something changing in me. I think I'm too close to it to talk about it in clear ways. Sometimes I realize that I've stopped singing and am just blessing Jesus. Sometimes I realize that a silly grin has crept onto my face.

I still get inhibited, of course. But these other moments are starting to get more and more common. When worship leaders say things about worship being "all about Jesus," I'm starting to have some idea of what they're talking about.

It's a fun process.

You could say I almost feel free. Not just free to cry out with the pains and ugly truth of reality. Not just free to run and fall at Jesus' feet.

But I feel free, too, to worship him as he helps me deal with these sins of mine.

Admitting how bad our sin is does not muddy the

grace of Jesus. Recognizing the true smell of sin brings it into full light for the first time. It compels us toward true worship and love. It frees us from the mediocre worship toward which these lies of "lite" sin have compelled us for too long.

Those who are forgiven much do, indeed, love much.

STINGING BLISS

When I was in third grade

I picked up two baby rattlesnakes with my dirty fingers
lay down in the deep green grass
and played with them all afternoon.

I danced on deep frozen ponds,
rode strange horses bareback and barefoot
and set the Appalachian Mountains on fire.

Then I stapled two of my fingers together.
And it hurt.
And I bled all over my teacher's desk.
And I cried in front of the class.

15

Know

> You will know the truth, and the truth
> will make you free.
> JOHN 8:31 NRSV

It's hard to have clarity these days.

Our world defies clarity.

And the enemy *detests* clarity. Only likes lies. Jesus knew this, of course. In Jesus' estimation, *he was a murderer from the beginning, and has nothing to do with the truth, because there is no truth in him. When he lies, he speaks according to his own nature, for he is a liar and the father of lies* (John 8:44 NRSV).

I think the enemy must take joy in our inability to correctly discern what we're choosing. He must love the false smell of sin that permeates our newspapers and classrooms and even our church buildings a lot of the time.

Sin is fun. God's way is boring and repressive. This has always been our enemy's favorite lie. Why bother with outright, blatant attacks when you can simply woo and undermine?

> Now the serpent was more crafty than any other wild
> animal that the LORD God had made. He said to the
> woman, "Did God say, 'You shall not eat from any tree
> in the garden?' " (Genesis 3:1 NRSV)

Did you see it right there in his very first attack on humanity? From the get-go the enemy's strategy is to make God out as the repressive one. *Did God say you can't eat anything good at all? Humph. God is such a prude. How boring! And you listen to him?!*

The woman doesn't fall immediately, though. She puts up a small fight.

> And the woman said to the serpent, "We may eat of the fruit of the trees of the garden; but God said, 'You shall not eat of the fruit of the tree which is in the midst of the garden, neither shall you touch it, lest you die.' "
> (Genesis 3:2-3)

Eve reasserts the true reality of things: God is generous and provides bountiful gifts. He isn't trying to keep us from good, fun things; he's providing all we could ever want. And his command to leave one tree alone? His first-ever "mark" that separates what is our target and what is outside of that target? That's to keep us from dying! That's to save us and keep us safe. It's a *good* thing!

Eve was right, of course. But Satan kept after her with that same lie, which he apparently has never tired of using since (and which we have never tired of falling for).

> But the serpent said to the woman, "You will not die; for God knows that when you eat of it your eyes will be opened, and you will be like God, knowing good and evil.' " (Genesis 3:4-5 NRSV)

And thus the subtle lies are planted within her and the seeds grow and she wonders. *Is God really so generous after all? And why not eat from that tree? I wonder what I've been missing out on all this time.*

And the enemy's small, subtle lie wins the first of many battles to come.

> So when the woman saw that the tree was good for food, and that it was a delight to the eyes, and that the tree was to be desired to make one wise, she took of its fruit and ate. (Genesis 3:6 NRSV)

If missing the mark is attractive, is *a delight to the eyes*, then why *should* she struggle against it? Just to appease this repressive God who has randomly forbidden certain attractive trees? To just keep from being *naughty*?

Well, there *was* that whole thing about death. But the enemy's subtle lies have a way of drowning out that graphic truth. And so Eve is utterly misled about what she's choosing between. She chooses the enemy's "truth" over God's. And thus her fall.

And at that moment the enemy was hooked on the technique he had just invented. *It's all about subtle deceptions, about misleading them as to what is good and attractive. Don't frighten them. Just softly woo them.*

Consider his attacks on Jesus. He skips the red cape, pointy horns and threatening pitchfork—no need for them! How does the enemy viciously attack Jesus? Offers him a chance to miraculously make bread. Offers him all the kingdoms of the world. Offers him a chance to command angels and impress all of Jerusalem (Luke 4:1-13).

Make no mistake about it, this subtle wooing is the enemy's calling card; it's his greatest strategy of attack. *Just confuse their picture of what they're choosing between.* This *has* to be his strategy, of course, because he just doesn't have better options for us. He has nothing better to offer, nothing that comes even close to the beautiful will of God.

What if Satan offered, *Choose a wonderful feast with God or empty, painful slavery with me*? That just wouldn't cut it. Humans aren't *that* dumb. So instead, Satan lies. *Choose a frigid, deprived, outdated way of living—or choose to live it up with these tasty, attractive, popular rides I offer, these so-called sins.*

IGNORANCE IS DANGEROUS

Jesus, of course, knew that Satan was the father of all lies. And so Jesus came (and still comes today) offering ultimate clarity and truth. And as the world's all-time greatest communicator (he is The Word, after all) he has a way of getting his point across.

Why else would he give us these graphic and gory images? He wants us to know. He wants us to know the truth more than he wants to avoid grossing us out and offending us.

And in this world of lies, we thank God for that.

His teachings on sin are not harsh, rather they are like smelling salts: they prick us and rouse us to consciousness. And why this rude awakening? So that we can shake off the dreams in our heads and clear away the blurry vision and see what's really going on around us . . . and in us.

And so he gives us the hard, naked truth to deal with. And it's a gift. It's a powerful gift.

In a world that strokes and encourages and profits from our coveting, it is a gift to us that Jesus comes and tells us that coveting is a disease. That it really chokes us and dizzies us.

In a world that strokes and encourages and profits from our lusting, it is a gift to us that Jesus comes and tells us that all lusting is spiritually significant, that it is adultery, that it blinds us and enslaves us.

In a world that strokes and encourages and profits from our sloth, it is a gift that Jesus comes and tells us that a life of rigorous activity in his kingdom is what brings life, and that a life of inactivity is an insult to God, our Creator and loving Father.

And in a world that strokes and encourages and profits from our selfishness, it is a gift that Jesus levels with us that true happiness will not come from binge buying, but from laying down our life for others—that selfishness enslaves us and becomes a cruel master, that a life lived only for ourselves is a fragile life, destined to fall apart.

Jesus' truth is strange. And it's very welcome! It is a good thing to be awake and know the truth. Ignorance is never bliss. Ignorance is ignorance. Ignorance is weakness. It is tragic and very, very dangerous.

And so Jesus comes with his stories of sawed-off hands and heavy millstones to free us from the lies we swim in. To open our eyes and shake us from this dull, sleepwalking world we live in.

His invitation to us today is the same as it was to the confused Jews at the Feast of Tabernacles: *Do not judge by appearances, but judge with right judgment* (John 7:24 NRSV).

Do not judge by appearances, but judge with right judgment. Good, common-sense advice, isn't it? And because of his clear teachings we *are* free to know. And in knowing comes power.

A high school junior gets confronted near her locker

one day by the gal she's been gossiping about. Now she has a choice. Satan whispers, *It's your choice. You can tell a small lie to cover up nicely and smooth over this conflict, or you can tell the "truth" and make everything awkward and rude.*

What should she choose? Doesn't "thou shalt not lie" seem silly and irrelevant at such a time?

But that's not the choice, and Jesus' words make that very clear. *The choice is yours,* Jesus says. *You can lie and sow seeds of dizziness and insult in your soul, or you can let your yes be yes and your no be no. You can deal honestly and find reconciliation and forgiveness.*

Jesus frees her from Satan's lies. And though lying may still tempt her, by knowing the truth about her choice she stands a much better chance of making a good choice.

The middle-aged man who gets a sizable raise also has a choice. The enemy whispers his version. *Listen, you can take care of yourself here and get some nice things. You deserve it! Or, sure, you can miss out on this chance by wasting your hard-earned money on some "charity"!*

What would *you* do, if these were your choices? I'd say it's time to turn up the "me" knob on life and do some fun buying! Right?

But Jesus comes with his painful, beautiful clarity on the matter.

> You have a choice. You can build up for yourself treasures on earth, where moth and rust consume and where thieves break in and steal. Or you can lay up for yourself treasures in heaven, where neither moth nor rust consumes and where thieves do not break in and steal. For where your treasure is, there will your heart be also. (Matthew 7:19-21)

Jesus' perspective includes eternity, includes the kingdom of God, and invites this man (if he will listen) to forsake short-sighted selfishness for something much greater.

The college freshman who lusts after the gal across the hall does not have to try to react like a lost young man in a dark room. He doesn't have to choose between some "innocent" flirting and being a "prude." He doesn't have to choose between lingering-eyes-and-lustful-thoughts and being-uptight-and-sexually-frustrated.

He can know. Jesus tells him the truth of sin, so this freshman does not have to be at the whim of what our culture would say. He is empowered by clarity. He can know that his real choice is between being a slave to lust and remaining free.

Jesus' teachings about the smell of sin free us to know. They free us from the enemy's attractive lies, they free us from the weight of our fallen culture's expectations, they free us to not judge by appearances but to make right judgments.

In my own life, I have been claiming this freedom more and more lately. When I'm faced with a temptation, all these teachings that I've been studying float before my eyes and I'm left with one important question in my heart and mind:

What am I really choosing between here?

Oh, sometimes I still choose poorly. I sin. But I feel much less under the thumb of the sins that have most tempted me in my life. And I'm distancing myself from them. Their power over me is growing fainter and fainter. It's a beautiful thing. It feels good to be awake.

It is good to know.

FOR LOVE OF MY COUCH

One day
I tried to throw away my used TV dinner
without getting up:

I remember distinctly the sick, muted sound of
    dirty aluminum
        thudding against
    the side of the hard plastic of the trash can.

The thick brown gravy dripped, slowly, down the
    side of the tan trash can
        as tight green peas
      went bouncing   in every direction
        across the white
linoleum floor.

I closed my eyes in disbelief.

When I opened them   my dog, Mutt,
    was spreading the gravy around
      with his large,
        red,
    slobbery tongue.

Then I watched him knock the trash can over.
With his tongue.

I yelled   and he ran back to the bedroom
    leaving a trail   of gravy-colored paw prints
      on the new
    Berber carpet.

I sighed.
And turned off the TV.

16

Sweat

> *The gate is narrow and the road is hard that leads to life.*
> MATTHEW 7:14 NRSV

The way is hard that leads to life? Hard. Hmm.

We're not so used to hard ways these days. We only want to sweat and exert ourselves as recreation—on our own time (and when we have suitable clothes to sweat in, thank you very much!).

It's not all our fault that we don't like to sweat. We live in an immediate age. We are taught to become indignant if we can't have something immediately. If it's taking too long we complain to the nearest manager or just drop it all together.

Some website is taking more than five seconds to pop up? Hmm. Forget it. Let's click over to that other site.

The fruit of living in an immediate culture? Our persistence muscles are atrophied. Our character is dulled. And we've become so enveloped in this soft, swivel-chair information age that we have no idea where a phrase like "elbow grease" could have had its origin.

We are soft.

And we follow a Jesus who calls us to intense, hard work.

When we smell the true smell of sin, we are like that woman caught in adultery (John 8:1-11). We are *guilty*, through and through. And we stand just as awkwardly as that accused woman at the utter mercy of this Jesus.

Now it's important for us to remember that there were *two* memorable moments for that woman.

The first was an unforgettable time of watching Jesus work a beautiful miracle for her. This was the time to feel vulnerable and helpless and whisper deep prayers, wondering what this famous carpenter would do and if the crowd would stone her after all. This was the time for her to watch the entire crowd walk away, one by one, removing her shame with each dusty step. This was the time to be left alone with Jesus and hear his beautiful voice whisper, *Neither do I condemn you.*

But it is so significant that their interaction didn't end there. There was a *second* powerful moment between Jesus and this woman. It was when Jesus looked her in the eyes and said, *Go and sin no more.*

(This is where the sweat comes in!)

Just like this woman, we need to cooperate with the work Jesus is doing inside of us. This will eventually and inevitably involve effort and passion and sweat on our part.

Jesus was very clear about this. *It's hard*, he said. The way to life is a hard way. It involves effort and strain and sweat and muscles and grunting. How do we "go and sin no more"? How do we cooperate with the work that Jesus is doing inside of us? With great effort, to be sure! Often by doing what, at first, seems difficult and awkward and unnatural.

DRASTIC CHANGES

We need to make drastic changes in our lives to keep temptation as far away as possible. If your hand causes you to sin, don't just slap it. Don't just give your hand a stern lecture. Jesus insists that you cut it off (Matthew 5:29)!

Jesus calls for drastic actions. Our question is not *How close to temptation can I get without giving in?* Our question needs to be *How far away can I run?*

Why else would Jesus ask the rich young ruler to give away all his possessions? Because for him they were a temptation. Get rid of them, Jesus instructed (Matthew 19:21).

And so we enter into the difficult task of making drastic changes to remove temptation. And the answers might not be easy to come by. We will need to put in some hard mental effort.

I know a vain woman who cut off her long, beautiful hair. (Her classmates were not impressed.)

I know a proud woman who covered up every mirror in her house for three months. (In the morning she had to ask her housemates if there was toothpaste on her face.)

I know a slothful young man who put a large hammer through the screen of his television. (Yeah, he had to figure out something else to do with his afternoons and evenings.)

And I know a lustful man who removed the Ethernet card from his computer and gave it to a friend for safe keeping. (Had to go way out of his way to check his e-mail from then on.)

Were any of these changes easy to make? Did their friends think they were weird for what they were doing?

Did they have a hard time explaining what they had done? No, yes, yes. It is difficult. Jesus promised it would be. It's tough to make drastic changes to remove temptations.

But was it worth it? Did the blessings outweigh the costs for these friends of mine? Oh, Jesus is never wrong. He doesn't lie. It was the best sweat they'd ever spent!

CONFESSION

Confession is a forgotten discipline these days.

It is a *discipline* precisely because we are sinners and Jesus knew that we would have sins to confess on a regular basis. It needs to be a regular, disciplined part of our life. If we don't confess on a regular basis, it's not because we're all put together, but rather because we're lying to ourselves (1 John 1:8). Confession is meant to be not an option but a discipline.

And it's a *forgotten* discipline because we hate to confess our sins. It's hard and awkward, and so we'd rather not. And no one really expects confession of us anyway. When we get together with our friends—even believing friends—we *share*, we *process*. But we don't necessarily expect each other to *confess*.

And why go against these well-established social expectations? It's just so much easier to share and sip our coffee and smile and nod and get on with our day. Why go against the flow and momentum of our easy relationships?

Because Jesus says that the way to life is, indeed, hard. And we want life. So we must confess our sins. And confession will shine light onto the dark places. It exposes hiding lies for the twisted things that they are. It leaves room for the Holy Spirit to move in us as our hearts become less guarded and more supple.

I suggest using short words. It's too easy to lose the truth in long-winded obfuscations. Use few words. Confess simply. And honestly.

ACCOUNTABILITY

Accountability? What an odd, out-of-place word that is, these days.

We need to rediscover this thing called *accountability*. We need to figure out how to have brothers and sisters who help keep us honest and encourage us. It's a simple, painful thing to do.

It's simple. Ask a few friends to ask you—directly and regularly—about your sins. And get ready. They might actually do it. (That's the painful part!)

Here are some helpful, though painful, hints born out of my own failures and weaknesses: Make sure they know you want them to initiate with you—this'll keep you honest. Make sure they know you want them to ask you the tough questions—and to ask those questions more than once. And make sure they'll ask, at the end, how you've lied to them during your confession. (If you're anything as slippery as me, you'll need faithful, honest, persistent friends!)

Make sure you thank them from time to time. And consider being that kind of friend to someone else. Be the kind of friend to others that you want them to be for you.

I know a man who asked a friend to call him daily to ask about a couple of specific sins he was really grappling with. (Kind of inconvenient—he had to be home at a certain time to get the calls.)

I know a few gals who came up with a subtle code word for one of their common temptations, so they wouldn't miss chances to hold each other accountable even if they were in public. (Sure, it took some foresight on their part.)

I know some young men who got up before the sun once a week to sit around on a cold cement dorm floor and simply confess their sins from the last week and thank God for his grace. (Sure, they were a little tired the rest of that day.)

I know a gal who asks her close friends the questions she wishes that they would ask her, even if those questions don't come up naturally in the course of conversation. (Sure, she gets some weird looks.)

True accountability is beautiful and powerful. Never easy and safe.

Drastic actions, confession, accountability—sounds like a lot of effort! Isn't there an easier way? Oh yes. Jesus said that, for sure, there was an easy way. The only problem? Well, in his own words, *There is a way that is easy that leads to death* (Matthew 7:13).

The path of least resistance is *not* always the best choice. Remember how to build a house? And how *not* to build a house? If we want to know what it's like to pursue life, then we need to imagine sweating a lot. That's what Jesus promised us it would be like.

This has been a new thing for me.

I've been a student a lot of my life. I like reading books and dealing in the world of ideas. I'm not so accustomed to hard work. Most days I have enough trouble just getting out of bed in the morning, let alone struggling and pressing and sweating against a tough enemy.

I like war movies and all the effort and heroics and inspiration involved. But from a safe distance. I've been softened and atrophied by this immediate-gratification culture I've grown up in. But Jesus is changing me.

I have found in Jesus' words a soberness that has compelled me to grow up and stop fooling around with my life. I am realizing that there are real consequences to the choices I make during the day.

There *is* a war going on, after all. And I'm right at the center of it. So I'm leaning hard against my temptations these days. I'm involving other people in the ugly areas of my life, because I need their help. Sure, I falter from time to time. But I am learning the sweet joy of a hard day's work.

There are some sins, some temptations that I had all but given up fighting in my life. But as I've been learning about Jesus' "take" on sin, I have been sobered into a true fight against these temptations.

And I'm finding that Jesus was not kidding when he said *Go and sin no more* to that woman caught in adultery. He really meant for her to go and live differently. He wanted her to see that conversion—big-time change—was possible for her. That she was meant for more than the life she had been living. That she deserved a life better than that. Well, not *deserved* it; a better life was what the God of love wanted for her.

You see, this call to hard work and sweat implies great hope. We strive against these sins knowing that it's Jesus who is both calling us to strive and enabling us to strive. It's Jesus who has freed us. And so we're not striving against the impossible, as the enemy would have us believe. It *is* possible to change. This year doesn't have to be like the last three years. *Change is possible.* In fact, change is mandatory.

And so I've confessed hard things. And I've invited friends to look out for me and pray for me and ask me hard questions.

There's just no way I can travel this hard way all on my own strength. But that's OK. In fact, that's wonderful. God isn't surprised at all that I falter and can't make it on my own.

In fact, we need to remember that all our efforts are taking place within the context of being helped by our great, alive God. Our sweat comes from cooperating with his work inside us. A patient must follow the doctor's instructions and prescriptions. A sheep must walk in the direction of the voice it hears. A released prisoner must stay away from the prison. Even a starving man being given bread and water must chew and swallow. All our efforts are within the safe, hopeful context of God's care for us.

Because of the smell of sin, we are free to cry out. We are free to love and worship Jesus. We are free to know.

And we are free to sweat.

My Kingdom for an Honest Friend

I wore a light blue
Cashmere tuxedo
to my high school prom.

And no one said a word.

17
Laugh

You fools!

LUKE 11:40 NRSV

The true way to respond to the smell of sin is to cry out and to worship. To know and to sweat.

But these aren't the *only* possible ways to respond to sin. Jesus knew that, and he knew how tempted we would be to respond poorly to sin. So Jesus took it upon himself to blow the cover on our poor plans for dealing with sin and to show them up, once and for all, as being utterly foolish. *Foolish.* Jesus had no qualms about deriding—outright making fun of—the foolish ways we sometimes respond to sin.

So he created caricatures. Quite ridiculous, almost cartoonish caricatures of how we're tempted to act. Not to belittle us, I think. But to point out in neon clarity how we should avoid responding to sin. These caricatures represent our temptations, and seeing them personified gives us the chance to see just how foolish they really are.

Like so many bright lighthouses marking the dangerous Coast of Foolishness, they stand, in neon silliness, to warn us of sharp rocks ahead. Let's heed his warning. Let's avoid the temptations that these caricatures represent. Let's not be fools.

PLANK EYE

Meet Plank Eye. He's a fool.

He's of average height and is decently good-looking. Or at least he used to be. It's hard to tell these days; sin is getting in the way of his face.

Plank Eye certainly believes in sin. In fact, he's very passionate about sin and getting rid of sin. Specifically, others' sins. To get an idea of this character, Jesus asked us to imagine someone with a log stuck in their eye (Matthew 7:3-5). That's a kind of disgusting thing for Jesus to ask us to imagine. It's pretty ludicrous, to be honest.

How does it fit in his eye exactly? Do his eyelid and whole eye socket stretch around the big log, or are they mutilated by the bloody log? Is the log sticking really far out of the eye? Two feet, seven feet? How am I supposed to imagine this person not just falling over from the weight of it all? And I wonder, is Plank Eye's nose being bent from the weight of the log? Can he still blink? Is the rough bark cutting up the skin around his eye?

It's hard to imagine, isn't it? And yet Jesus asks us to. In fact, he asks us to imagine something even worse.

If we can somehow get this cartoonishly grotesque Plank Eye pictured in our imagination, Jesus now asks us to imagine him trying to get a piece of dust out of someone else's eye.

I don't know about you, but I hate the thought of even a sane, surgically prepped doctor trying to get a speck out of my eye. It's *my* eye. I have policies about my eyes. No one else touches them, for example. It's nothing personal, it's just a policy.

And yet Mr. Plank Eye somehow notices a friend's eye has a speck in the corner of it. So he lumbers over—

swinging eye-plank and all—to get that speck out!

Disaster awaits. Does the friend get his head knocked around by the log as the "doctor" leans in? Does blood from the log-filled, grotesquely stretched eye fall onto the face of the friend?

Too many questions. All too ridiculous! Much too grotesque.

And yet Jesus says this is how we are tempted to respond to sin. Instead of crying out to Jesus and working hard on our sin, we are tempted to completely ignore the sin in our own lives (quite a task!) and focus on the small sins of others around us.

That is foolish, Jesus says. Utterly foolish.

Let's not do that. Let's not pretend our eyes are fine. Let's not bumble around with gross things hanging out of our faces. Let's deal with our own sin.

Then, in humility and gentleness, we will be in a much better place to help others with their own temptations and struggles.

Let's not be so occupied with the sins of others that we can't even see our own sin. Let's not cry "How dare you, you sinners!" without first crying out for our own real, tangible sins.

Let's not be the adulterous husband who is irate at "all those homosexuals out there!"

Let's not be the woman who enjoys flirting with her married neighbor but can't stand "those whores down on Broadway!"

Let's not be the racist college student who protests loudly against "those capitalist pigs who are destroying our planet!"

Let's not be the young man who regularly enjoys

lurid Internet sites but cringes in disgust while driving by "those nasty adult bookstores!"

Let's beware of praying prayers similar to the prayer of the Pharisee in Jesus' parable:

> God, I thank you that I am not like other people: thieves, rogues, adulterers, or even like this tax collector. I fast twice a week; I give a tenth of all my income. (Luke 18:11-12 NRSV)

When we sit down to list the sins that bug us, are they ever the sins we struggle so deeply with? Or are we quick to ignore the logs in our own eyes while focusing so intently and with such passion on the specks in the eyes of those around us?

Jesus never makes a hierarchy of sins. Sins of idolizing money are just as smelly as sexual sins. A "white lie" is just as insulting to our Father as cold-blooded murder. So the most important sins must always be our own. Our own.

Let the rich man whose idol is money sneer at the prostitute. Let the prostitute roll her eyes at that obvious slave of money.

And let them both be fools.

Let the adulterous patroness of the country club click her tongue at the pregnant teen who fills her water glass. Let the pregnant teen clear her throat at that mirror of a torrid soap opera.

And let them both be fools.

That is not our call; that is foolish. Let's not be fools.

CAMEL GUT

Meet Mr. Camel Gut. He's also a fool.

This fellow looks like . . . well, it's hard to tell exactly what he once must have looked like. The camel he swallowed kind of blurs what used to be the outline of his body.

Unlike Plank Eye, this fellow knows that he has sins and temptations and weaknesses. And he is very purposeful, careful and diligent in dealing with them. A humble man. He is disciplined and watchful, keeping an eye out for temptations at all times.

Only problem? While he uses his microscope on these known areas of his life, there are other, mammoth issues that he's totally ignoring. Seems silly, doesn't it, to be so careful in some areas and totally foolish in others? Yeah.

Jesus said it was like straining out a gnat, but swallowing a camel (Matthew 23:24). Now that's foolish!

Can you see the picture Jesus is asking us to imagine? Can you picture the bloated Mr. Camel Gut leaning over his soup, looking intently for a stray gnat that might possibly have fallen in? A study in discipline and watchfulness, right? Except for the fact that there's a huge camel shape coming out of his distended stomach!

What would it be like to "unknowingly" swallow a camel anyway? Unknowingly? I can imagine swallowing a gnat by accident, but a *camel?* A ridiculous picture dreamed up by Jesus—to teach us something.

Let's not be like that.

If we feel we are satisfied with our dealings with sin, if we feel diligent and careful in areas of temptation, let's be wary lest there are some huge areas of sin going unnoticed and not being dealt with!

Let the bitter old woman continue to fervently guard

her lips from a drop of alcohol. And let the bitterness in her heart rot and fester.

Let the jealous teenager dutifully keep herself from ever cussing again. And let the jealousy slowly enslave her until even seemingly kind words from her mouth are laced with venom.

Let the prayer-less pastor give wonderful sermons. And let him wander farther and farther from his Father.

Let's beware of blind spots, of habits that are so long-standing that we don't even see them any more.

Let's ask the friends we trust, *Do you see any camel shapes coming out of my gut? Do you see sin in me that I don't notice?*

If we don't do this we will be deceived into believing all is well, while camels slowly slide into our small intestines.

MRS. SHINY CORPSE

Meet Mrs. Shiny Corpse. She's a fool.

Oh, she's a pretty enough gal. That'll probably be the first thing that strikes you when you meet her. The second thing, though, is that weird smell that you can't quite place until it's too late and you've sat down right next to her!

Oh, she loves being clean! She scrubs and shines and bleaches and sprays. But there's still that odd smell . . .

This is the woman without apparent sin. To all who meet her she is the picture of righteousness. No protruding camel shapes. No logs to be seen. All is carefully in its place, and all is clean and shiny.

Her face and manners sparkle. She is the woman the pastor refers to often in his sermons. She is an example of all that is decent and respectable and joyful.

Only problem? On the inside, she's rotting.

A silly thing to be clean and shiny on the outside but rotting within. Who, in their right mind, after a great Thanksgiving meal, would carefully polish the outside of the silver gravy boat and put it away on the shelf until next year's holidays—without washing the leftover gravy out of the inside?

No one. No one in their right mind would do that, right? We'd think them a fool! Well, so did Jesus.

> Now you Pharisees clean the outside of the cup and of the dish, but inside you are full of greed and wickedness. You fools! (Luke 11:39-40 NRSV)

Jesus thinks we'd be fools to fuss over our appearances and yet not deal with what's going on inside.

How sobering to hear Jesus' words to the handsome, dignified scribes and Pharisees:

> Woe to you, scribes and Pharisees, hypocrites! For you are like whitewashed tombs, which on the outside look beautiful, but inside they are full of the bones of the dead and of all kinds of filth. So you also on the outside look righteous to others, but inside you are full of hypocrisy and lawlessness. (Matthew 23:27-28 NRSV)

The goal is not to appear righteous. That is never our goal or hope. How foolish to respond to sin by scrubbing and faking and acting. How foolish.

Let the selfish man who lives for his possessions smile, and tell jokes, and slap his colleagues on the back. And let him rot, quietly and sadly, from within.

Let the woman who's had an affair treat her husband

well and dote on him and make better dinners than she ever has. And let the covered up sin fester from within.

Let the young couple who has gone too far physically but is too embarrassed to talk about it with each other keep up all their social graces. And let the heavy hammer of shame and secret guilt slowly drive a wedge between them and everyone around them.

Let the envious young lady win applause and public recognition for her numerous volunteer activities. And let her life become emotionally off-balance and teeter on the edge of collapse.

Anytime we find ourselves with a clean outside and a questionable inside but refuse to do anything but feverishly polish the outside, Jesus has a very definite opinion about us. And he's never been shy about expressing it.

YOU AND I

Let's not be fools. Let's not concern ourselves with appearances, but with reality.

I'm afraid I'm really good at being a fool.

Camel Gut, Plank Eye, Shiny Corpse: I think I've one-upped them all in the business of foolishness. I've swallowed a camel or two in my day, and I must say my exterior (though I lean more toward khaki and flannel than silver and gold) has gotten quite a bit of polishing.

But Jesus is freeing me. All these teachings on sin that have been haunting me have indeed provided intense conviction, but I'm finding there is great freedom in the brave clarity of calling a spade a spade—or a fool a fool.

Why does Jesus feel it necessary to use such graphic and comic images to describe me? Because it's true. I am tragic, and even comic, in my sin. And Jesus invites me to shake my head and laugh at myself, and to forsake this foolishness.

I think Jesus painted these caricatures with bright, comical neon colors so we could avoid them at all costs. Camel Gut, Plank Eye and Shiny Corpse are like bright lighthouses on the dangerous Coast of Foolishness. They are perched on sharp rocks and cry out to us, "Don't come near!" They call out to us from across the centuries to warn us of a land, and lots of dangerous rocks, that we should at all costs avoid.

I can know that being overly concerned with others' sins while not too concerned about my own is a dangerous place to be. I can know to avoid blind spots in my life by asking others if they see any humped animal shapes coming from my intestines. I can take pause when I notice myself opening the can of polish a lot. And I can laugh at these temptations and thereby rob them of some of their luster.

It's a gift that Jesus brightly established a lighthouse of warning on the rocks of foolishness. It is not a good place to go.

So, let's not go there. We're free to name it for what it really is: *The Coast of Foolishness*. And we're free to forsake it for better ground.

OVERHEARD IN THE
DISNEYLAND PARKING LOT

Why do parents
walk everywhere
so slow?

I just want to run!

18

Run

> *Let us also lay aside every weight, and*
> *sin that clings so closely, and let us run*
> *with perseverance the race that is set*
> *before us, looking to Jesus, the pioneer*
> *and perfecter of our faith.*
>
> HEBREWS 12:1-2 NRSV

It is essential to note, after reading an entire book on sin, that sin is not the point. It never has been.

The point, the *call* of the gospel, is a call into life.

Again, the image for understanding our life with God can never be this frigid classroom where we try to sit still and avoid upsetting the teacher. A classroom is not a handy analogy. It's not a *biblical* analogy! Neither is the picture of a kill-joy God punishing those who indulge in exciting sins.

Rather, what we find throughout the Gospels is that Jesus graciously calls us into life. Into an amazing, surprising, costly, beautiful life. We should read these Gospels with joy and pursue, doggedly, the life we find there.

It's just like basketball. Playing a game of hoops is not about out-of-bounds. Basketball is never all about the traveling and fouls and double dribbles. Basketball is about the scoring, the tight dribbling, the behind-the-back pass for an alley-oop dunk! The point isn't the rules that keep the game in control and keep people from getting hurt. The rules are necessary. But the point is the game!

The verse from Hebrews 12 that opened this book and heads this chapter does not end, we must note, after the words "Let us lay aside all these sins which so easily cling to us." No. That's just the start of the sentence. Why do we lay aside all these sins? "SO THAT WE MAY RUN!"

We struggle against sins so that we may engage in the purposeful adventure that God has for us in Jesus: the race that is set before us! We're made to run. We're made for active righteousness.

Sin does smell bad. (As we've seen, Jesus wants us to be very clear on that matter.) But what should primarily preoccupy our theological noses is the fresh air of grace. In it we detect the sweet scent of righteousness—a scent Jesus spent even more time and energy and vivid words describing.

We can't help but get whiffs of this heavenly scent of righteousness in the exact same word pictures we've been considering throughout this book: Our call is to experience deep, intimate, familiar relationship with God (not to spit at him in rebellion). We are meant to live connected to Jesus, the true vine, who provides us with the soul nutrients that we need to live (not to commit spiritual suicide). Our lives are meant to be lived in clarity and light, lived with the simplicity and beauty of a sheep following its master's beloved voice (not as blind, dizzy, lost sheep).

Jesus' graphic descriptions of the reality of sin are matched—and even surpassed—by his vivid, provocative, beautiful descriptions of what life in him can be like.

Let's save ourselves for that. Let's not succumb to the fetid life to which our enemy calls us. We are meant for so much more. Our Father has created us for so much more. So let us pursue that fragrant life with all we have. It's the wisest thing we could ever do with our time here on earth.

This little book on sin? It's just a small theological correction. A simple reminder that this world does not know the truth about sin. It's a call to listen to Jesus' graphic teachings on the matter—and to believe him.

It's a call to freedom. To reap the fruits of a life lived eyes wide open. To breathe in the fresh air of clean, true grace and to be smothered no longer by the stench that has surrounded us for so long.

And it is (I hope) an embarrassing exposé on the tired old strategies of our enemy.

We have Jesus. We have the words of the One who was there when we were created. We have his Spirit, our blessed Counselor, who walks each step with us.

We don't have to be bullied around by these old sins. We don't have to follow the deceptive lies of the enemy as we make our daily choices.

We are free to be wise.

But wisdom must never look like some hooded monk perched in meditation on a mountaintop. Wisdom looks like crying and mourning. Wisdom involves breathless worship. Wisdom is aerobic. It's a bunch of hard work.

If we pursue wisdom we should expect to look very different from the world around us. We should expect to feel different emotions than we are accustomed to and experience a prayer life that might not look like what we now know.

If we want to be wise, we'll find ourselves leaning on those around us. And the world we walk in will start looking much different than it ever has.

And Jesus will call us blessed.

And the enemy will growl, for wisdom exposes the enemy's rotting lies for what they really are.

May we all run joyfully in this blessed wisdom.

Afterword

> *Because of this many of his disciples*
> *turned back and no longer went about*
> *with him. So Jesus asked the twelve,*
> *"Do you also wish to go away?"*
> *Simon Peter answered him, "Lord,*
> *to whom can we go? You have the*
> *words of eternal life."*
>
> JOHN 6:66-68 NRSV

Over the past several months I have lived rather bothered.

These word pictures that Jesus paints have roused me to consciousness. To be honest, at times it has felt more like an abrupt shaking than a gentle rousing. It has hurt.

There have been moments when I've longed for my comfortable old lies about sin, like some little child crying for his familiar, well-worn blanket. But I am left with the sober reality that these harsh images of sin are Jesus' words, Jesus' pictures. So I've stuck with it. And (not too surprisingly) I've found that it's entirely worth it.

It feels good to be awake. It's a welcome breath of fresh air to not be fooled so much by the enemy. It's tiring and scary *and wonderful* to cry and worship and sweat and know.

It has been—as is always the case when submitting to Jesus—a beautiful thing.

But please don't take my word for it. That is not my intention or hope.

You see, there's a reason I have looked almost exclusively at the Gospels throughout these pages. Because, when all is said and done, it doesn't matter what some skinny young author writes about sin. Ultimately, this short stack of pages you are holding right now doesn't matter at all. (Knowing that, I just want to point out that I did try to keep it short!)

What must ultimately concern us are the words and life of our dear Jesus. We must always be *looking to Jesus, the pioneer and perfecter of our faith* (Hebrews 12:2 NRSV).

May we delve into his teachings on sin, then. May his Spirit breathe clarity and conviction into our days. And may we find ourselves so leaning upon him and his words, with every inch of our lives, that we find this rare blessedness that he speaks of.

May we wrestle with Jesus. And may we wind up smelling more like him.

—